Beyond Bullet Points:
Using Microsoft® PowerPoint® to Create Presentations That Inform, Motivate, and Inspire

Cliff Atkinson

PUBLISHED BY
Microsoft Press
A Division of Microsoft Corporation
One Microsoft Way
Redmond, Washington 98052-6399

Library of Congress Control Number 2004118057

Printed and bound in the United States of America.

2 3 4 5 6 7 8 9   QWT   9 8 7 6 5

Distributed in Canada by H.B. Fenn and Company Ltd.

A CIP catalogue record for this book is available from the British Library.

Microsoft Press books are available through booksellers and distributors worldwide. For further information about international editions, contact your local Microsoft Corporation office or contact Microsoft Press International directly at fax (425) 936-7329. Visit our Web site at www.microsoft.com/learning/. Send comments to *mspinput@microsoft.com*.

Microsoft, Microsoft Press, OneNote, Outlook, PowerPoint, and Visio are either registered trademarks or trademarks of Microsoft Corporation in the United States and/or other countries.

The example companies, organizations, products, domain names, e-mail addresses, logos, people, places, and events depicted herein are fictitious. No association with any real company, organization, product, domain name, e-mail address, logo, person, place, or event is intended or should be inferred.

Acquisitions Editors: Hilary Long and Juliana Atkinson
Project Editor: Sandra Haynes
Technical Editor: Steve Sagman
Editorial and Production: Studioserv (www.studioserv.com)

Body Part No. X11-08053

To my partner, Andrew Harmon,
and my parents, Reuben and Hildegund Atkinson.

Contents

Chapter 4

Preparing and Planning Your Storyboard   77

Chapter 5

Choosing a Design Style for Your Storyboard   113

Chapter 6

Expanding Your Graphical Options   149

Chapter 7
Bringing Your Story to Life   181

Acknowledgments

My special gratitude to Juliana Aldous Atkinson and the team at Microsoft Press, who graciously invited me to write this book. If these ideas reach a wider audience and make a positive difference, it is because you made this book possible.

Thanks to my editing team of Sandra Haynes, Steve Sagman, and Jennifer Harris. Your guidance and thorough review greatly improved the clarity of the book. Thanks to Steve Few for reviewing chapters and to Richard E. Mayer for reviewing the research material in Appendix A.

A salute to the many people whose ideas have inspired or influenced parts of this book, including Aristotle, Henry Boettinger, Jim Bonnet, Syd Field, Kathleen Hall Jamieson, Richard E. Mayer, Scott McCloud, Robert McKee, and Barbara Minto. Thanks to the many people who have graciously accepted my invitation to be interviewed about Microsoft Office PowerPoint for my newsletter, including Seth Godin, Bob Horn, Guy Kawasaki, Larry Lessig, Don Norman, Michael Schrage, John Seely Brown, and Nathan Shedroff. Thanks to Till Voswinckel for our ongoing conversation. A special thanks to William C. Chittick for translating the thirteenth-century writings of Jalal al-Din Rumi and Ibn al-Arabi, which have been an endless source of inspiration.

And last but not least, a special thanks to my friends and fellow members of my local speaking club, Toastmasters Executive 412, who provided the welcoming community where many of the ideas and insights in this book came to life.

Introduction

Would a Microsoft Office PowerPoint presentation without bullet points still be a PowerPoint presentation?

That's a hard question to answer these days, because wherever people gather for presentations, you're sure to see the same predictable format on the screen of the meeting room, slide after slide. The conventional bullet points approach in presentations has such a strong grip on our collective consciousness that it produces remarkably consistent results across organizations, professions, and even cultures.

If you're like most people who use PowerPoint, creating a presentation starting with a series of bullet points is probably second nature. Bullet points are easy to write, and they make creating slides a breeze. When you show them on screen during a presentation, they quickly remind you of what you want to say and provide a record that you've shown the audience the information you intended. Like PowerPoint presentations themselves, bullet points are so much a part of our everyday lives, it's hard to imagine how things could be any different.

But although bullet points make it easy for us to create slides, they don't always make it easy for audiences to understand what we want to say. Growing numbers of people are expressing a sense of frustration with the conventional bullet points approach, and they're expressing themselves in a wide range of forums including discussion groups, surveys, books, essays, articles and blog postings. What they're saying, basically, is that slides filled with bullet points create obstacles between presenters and audiences. You might want to be natural and relaxed when you present, but people say that bullet points make the atmosphere formal and stiff. You might aim to be clear and concise, but people often walk away from these presentations feeling confused and unclear. And you might intend to display the best of your critical thinking on a screen, but people say that bullet points "dumb down" the important discourse that needs to happen for our society to function well.

Somewhere in our collective presentation experience, we're not connecting the dots between presenters and audiences by using the conventional bullet points approach. This issue is of rising concern not only to individuals and audiences— even the major players of large organizations are taking notice of the problem. It seems that in every location where people meet, from small meeting rooms to board rooms to conference halls, people want a change.

As a presenter, what are your options? Isn't the bullet points approach all that's possible with PowerPoint? In fact, there's something you *can* do. You can tell a story instead. If what people are saying about bullet points is true, we can interpret their complaints as a symptom of something that's gone missing. It's almost as if the pendulum has swung too far in the direction of bulleted lists, charts, and graphs to the point where we've lost the balance that we need to make us feel connected to one another. In this fast-paced culture of change and complexity in which we live, people understandably yearn for a return to the basics of human connection, inspiration, and common purpose. That's exactly what a story can offer.

The concept of a story has been emerging as a hot topic in organizations, but why would a story be more of an appropriate model for presentations? In most presentation contexts, we don't gather simply to tell anecdotes to entertain one another—although a personal story can be a powerful technique to support a point. Rather, presentations should help us to discuss and decide on the issues that shape our lives and our organizations. Presentations are different from personal anecdotes because they deal with complex issues and usually involve the reasoning and logic that's essential to informed decision-making.

We can strike a balance between the benefits of storytelling and the need for reasoning by applying a specific type of story *structure* to the complex requirements of a presentation. We can reach back into history to rediscover the classical foundation of both storytelling and persuasion then apply those concepts to PowerPoint presentations today to dramatic effect. A persuasive story structure is strong enough to hold whatever your presentations demand, including the rigor of your critical thinking and the sophisticated media techniques audiences expect. Applying this type of story structure to your PowerPoint presentations is the heart of the three-step approach described in this book, which introduces a completely new alternative to the conventional bullet points approach.

The Beyond Bullet Points approach to PowerPoint presentations has roots in many sources, including classical philosophy, contemporary media techniques, and recent research related to the way people learn from multimedia. It draws from these inspirations and more, and interprets them all through the lens of a process you can use to produce a presentation. This book doesn't dwell on the theory behind the ideas, but instead embeds the ideas into every step of the process.

Chapter 1 introduces a fictional scenario in which you're faced with the challenge of transforming a presentation using the conventional bullet points approach into a new presentation without bullet points. Chapters 2 and 3 guide you through the step 1 of the Beyond Bullet Points approach: *writing a script to focus your ideas.* Chapters 4 through 6 walk you through step 2: *storyboarding your script to clarify your ideas.* And Chapter 7 introduces step 3: *producing your script to engage your audience.*

Beginning with Chapter 2, each chapter ends with 10 advanced tips that you can use to enhance the key ideas in each of the chapter. (When you first read the book, you can skim through these tips, and then return to them later when you're ready to put them into practice.) This book is designed to be a practical guide that you keep close at hand while you work on PowerPoint presentations, as well as a source of ongoing inspiration.

The heart of this book is that it's really about people communicating with people. By using a commonly available software tool to help you to do that, you can find focus, clarity, and engagement. I hope you'll find that and much more in this book, as you make and tell your own presentation stories *beyond bullet points.*

About the Author

CLIFF ATKINSON is a leading authority on how to improve communications across organizations using Microsoft PowerPoint. He is a popular keynote speaker, a writer, and an independent management consultant whose clients include companies ranking in the top five of the Fortune 500. He is president of Sociable Media in Los Angeles.

As a captain in the U.S. Air Force, Cliff earned the title of best commentary writer in the Department of Defense; after his service, he held marketing and consulting positions for a couple of start-up companies in San Francisco during the dot-com boom. He holds a B.A. in English and journalism from Baylor University in Texas and an M.B.A. in international business from Richmond–The American International University in London.

Cliff teaches at UCLA Extension, is a senior contributor for the MarketingProfs newsletter, and is author of the Beyond Bullets blog, at *www.beyondbullets.com*.

Chapter 1: Moving Beyond Bullet Points: A Three-Step Approach

In this chapter, you will:

1. Analyze a typical presentation scenario.

2. Consider some of the problems that bullet points present.

3. Learn the importance of a story.

4. Survey the Hollywood process for producing media.

5. Review a three-step approach to moving beyond bullet points.

Giving a presentation can be a challenge for anyone. But it's even more challenging when you have to give a presentation to the board of directors of your organization next week and they've specifically asked you not to use "boring" bullet points for your slides. What do you do?

The thought of public speaking strikes fear in the hearts of most people. Not only do you have to prepare to speak in front of a group of people you don't know, you also have very little time to figure out what to say and how to say it effectively. Where do you begin?

This book can help. It introduces the Beyond Bullet Points approach, which will help you to produce any presentation using Microsoft Office PowerPoint without relying on bullet points. You will be guided, step by step, through the makeover of a single presentation so that you can see the approach in action. Based on a blend of classical ideas and modern technology, this three-step approach helps you focus your ideas, clarify them, and bring them to life for your audience. You can easily apply the techniques in this book to any presentation—whether you're an entrepreneur, a salesperson, an educator, a professional speaker, a student, an engineer, or a scientist—because they're for anyone who uses PowerPoint to communicate.

SEE ALSO As you follow the specific example of this scenario, you can also visit www.sociablemedia.com to see examples of other types of presentations you might give for other purposes, including training, education, fund raising, sales, and more.

The benefits of this approach go much deeper than the aesthetics of your slides. You'll not only produce more engaging visuals, but at each step along the way, you'll also grow more confident as a speaker, more sure of your message, and more connected with your audience. There's plenty to say about the ideas underlying this new approach, but you have a presentation to give next week to the board of directors, so let's jump right into the specific scenario.

Introducing the Scenario

This book will guide you through the process of redesigning an existing PowerPoint presentation using the tools and techniques of the Beyond Bullet Points approach. As you see the approach unfold, you can use this fictional scenario to help you learn the approach and apply it to your own presentations.

Here's the scenario you face—it's your first day at your new job as the director of marketing for Contoso Pharmaceuticals in Los Angeles. You've wanted to work at Contoso for a long time, so you're thrilled to be here. When you get to your desk and turn on your laptop computer, there's an e-mail waiting for you from your boss, Michelle Alexander, the vice president of marketing.

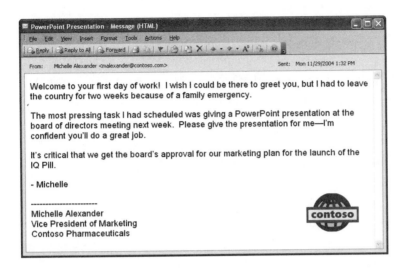

The *IQ Pill* is Contoso Pharmaceutical's new breakthrough drug that instantly doubles the intelligence of anyone who takes it. It's a miracle of science that has been under development for years and is finally ready to be released.

The successful launch of the IQ Pill is crucial to your company's financial performance next quarter, so the board has dedicated an hour of its meeting next week to review and discuss the marketing plan you will present. But there's a glitch. When you check your voice mail there's a message from Contoso's CEO, Chris Gray:

> "Welcome aboard! I was sorry to hear about Michelle's situation, and I hope everything is all right. Michelle told me she forwarded to you the materials for the PowerPoint presentation you're going to give to the board next week. I reviewed the presentation with her yesterday, and I approved the marketing plan—I think she did a great job. But we have a little problem. The board members have been giving me a hard time about our PowerPoint presentations, and I agree that the presentations can be unfocused, wordy, and dull. They've told me that they don't want

to see any 'boring' bullet points at next week's meeting. They still want presenters to use PowerPoint, but they want the visuals to be focused, clear, and engaging. Take a look at our current PowerPoint file, and let's set up a meeting for Wednesday so that you can show me what you can do to improve it. See you then."

So, its your first day on the job and you've already been given these challenges:

1   Give a presentation to the board next week using PowerPoint.

2   Use no bullet points.

3   Be focused, clear, and engaging.

You expected to hit the ground running in your new job at Contoso, but you weren't quite expecting your first day to be anything like this.

A good way to start your new project is to step back for a moment and analyze the situation. Why would an audience ask presenters to move beyond bullet points in the first place? What were the Contoso board members really saying when they told the CEO that the current approach is producing "unfocused, wordy and dull" presentations? To find the answers to your questions, you go to the source: the current PowerPoint file that's waiting in your e-mail inbox. You locate and open the Contoso marketing plan PowerPoint presentation so you can analyze its contents next.

Analyzing the Problem

Analyzing a PowerPoint file outside of its presentation context can be difficult because you're missing some important pieces of information. You don't know exactly what the presenter intends to achieve with the presentation. You also don't know how the presenter actually works with the PowerPoint slides during the live presentation or how the audience responds. But even without this context, you can still ask three basic questions about every PowerPoint presentation to analyze its effectiveness.

Three Analysis Questions

1. In Slide Sorter view Can I see the focus of the presentation by reading only the slide titles?

2. In Notes Page view Does this presentation balance my spoken words and projected visuals?

3. In Normal view Will the slides look interesting to my audience?

Let's see how you'd answer each of these questions when you look at the Contoso PowerPoint presentation.

Can I See the Focus of the Presentation by Reading Only the Slide Titles?

The first question to ask about any set of PowerPoint slides is whether they help the viewer quickly understand the main idea of the entire presentation. At this initial stage of your analysis, reviewing the specifics of individual slides is not as important as seeing how the slides work together as a whole. To take a look at the big picture of any presentation, click **View, Slide Sorter** to display thumbnail-size versions of all of your slides in a single view, as shown in Figure 1-1.

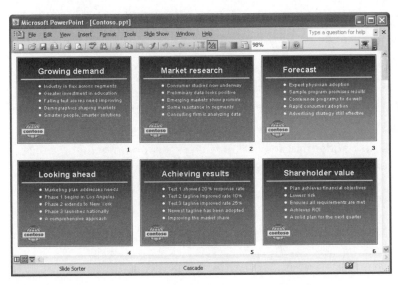

Figure 1-1 *Slide Sorter view of the Contoso PowerPoint presentation*

As you review your slides in this view, ask yourself, "Can I see the focus of this presentation by reading only the slide titles?" When you review any presentation in Slide Sorter view, you should be able to determine the main idea of the presentation at a glance. If you can't confidently grasp the focus of your presentation in Slide Sorter view, your audience will not confidently grasp the focus of your ideas either. In the example shown in Figure 1-1, the main idea is as hard to find as a needle in a bullet point haystack.

The titles of these example slides don't help you see what is most important because they are *category headings*—like those you see in almost all PowerPoint presentations. These generic headings designate a general category of information for a slide but offer little about the specific information the slide contains. A category heading like "Growing demand" is actually an information placeholder that asks the implied question "What information belongs to this category?" You naturally answer that question by listing the category items with bullet points.

A category heading can help you quickly brainstorm a list of information, but as you can see here, it does nothing to help you quickly understand what is the most important information on a single slide or *across* the slides in a presentation. When you read the three headings in this example ("Growing demand," "Market research," "Forecast"), they really don't say anything specific. To find out what the headings mean, you need to invest extra time you don't have to connect all the dots of the bullet points below the headings.

REMEMBER Using generic category headings as the titles of your slides makes it difficult for both you and your audience to see the focus of your presentation.

Category headings put an extra burden on you and your audience as you both struggle to see the focus of your ideas through the slides in your presentation. As your audience views these headings and their corresponding stacks of bulleted lists, slide after slide, it's no wonder that they find the presentation unfocused, hard to understand, and overwhelmed with unnecessary details.

Does This Presentation Balance My Spoken Words and Projected Visuals?

The next question to ask of any presentation is how well it balances your spoken words and projected visuals. You can analyze a presentation using these criteria by looking at the PowerPoint file from a little-used perspective called Notes Page view. To review your file from this angle, select any slide and click **View, Notes Page** to see a view similar to Figure 1-2.

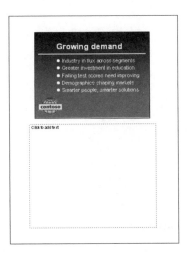

Figure 1-2   *The Notes Page view of a selected slide from the Contoso presentation.*

In Notes Page view, the top half of the screen displays the slide that appears on the screen during a presentation. The text box below, which does not appear on screen during a presentation, can be used to write down the words you will speak while you show this slide. In this example, as in most PowerPoint presentations, all the information has been squeezed into the slide area above, while the notes area below was ignored. The result is that the relationship between your spoken words and projected visuals is not addressed.

Because half of the available real estate for information is not used, the slide area becomes the single place that holds both spoken words and projected images. This creates a scarcity of resources in the slide area, which predictably produces overloaded slides. Words will usually take priority over visuals, so you will tend to see slides filled with text—which is what the Contoso board noticed. Visuals added to these already crowded slides will usually shrink to the size of postage stamps so that they can squeeze between the boxes of text. These dynamics produce slides that are overly complex and difficult to understand. The result is usually information overload for your audience.

Always remember that no PowerPoint slide exists in a vacuum. You are standing there speaking to your audience while you project the slide. That means that you must effectively plan how your spoken words and projected images relate to each other. If you don't balance what you say with what you show, you are certain to create an imbalance in understanding for your audience.

REMEMBER Ignoring the notes area forces you to squeeze all of your information into the slide area.

Does This Look Interesting to My Audience?

The last question to ask about your presentation is what impact your slides will have on your audience. Audience response can be difficult to predict, of course, because your audience is not present during your analysis. But you can get a rough idea of how things will look to them if you click View, Normal to display your slides in Normal view. This time, when you look at a slide, imagine that your audience is in the room viewing it, as in this example:

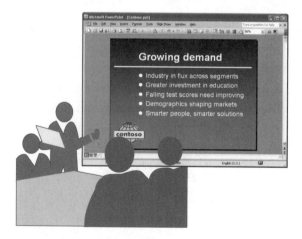

This technique will give you a sense of what your viewers will experience when they see this slide. Unfortunately, the view in this example doesn't look engaging. What your audience experiences is exactly what *you* experience when bullet points appear on a screen. What was once interesting suddenly becomes dull. The atmosphere becomes formal and stiff, and relaxed discussion stops. It's almost as if bullet points take aim at whatever is interesting and lively in a room and silently kill it.

In your analysis, you've already noted some of the roots for these common audience symptoms, including a lack of focus and overloaded slides. Another obstacle is the monotonous background of the slides. As in most PowerPoint presentations, these example Contoso slides were created using a design template with a single, predesigned background. Using a single background gives slides a uniform look, but it also prevents you from using a wide range of design techniques to visually highlight the most important information on single slides or across slides. It can also make your slides appear repetitive or tedious, which might cause boredom and inhibit understanding.

These problems can create confusion and frustration for an audience when a presenter simply reads bullet points from slides to an audience. The most common audience response to this situation is, "If you're going to just read me the slides, why do I need to be there? Just e-mail them to me!"

Showing and reading bullet points to an audience undermines the purpose of presentations. People attend presentations to learn about a topic as it is explained by another person. When you read bullet points, the slide is doing the talking, not you. This becomes a counterproductive exercise that can waste both your time and your audience's. Being chained to the sequence of bullet points in your slides can also severely constrain your ability to demonstrate confidence in your topic, express your personality, and make a real connection with your audience.

> **REMEMBER** Reading your slides to the audience constrains your ability to demonstrate your confidence, express your personality, and make a real connection.

But it doesn't have to be this way. The Contoso board has given you an opportunity to use your analysis to transform your PowerPoint presentation beyond bullet points. When you close your PowerPoint file, you think for a moment about what you have to do. You're confident that you have good information in your current presentation, so your main challenge is to present that information in a new way that makes it easier to understand. You have a great deal at stake here because you want to make a good first impression in your new job and you want to help Contoso meet its financial goals next quarter with the successful marketing launch of the IQ Pill.

But what strategy will help you to move the Contoso PowerPoint presentation beyond bullet points and make it focused, clear, and engaging? To find out you need to step back from PowerPoint for a moment to see the bigger presentation context.

Selecting a Strategy

One of the reasons the Contoso board of directors, like most audiences, wants to move beyond bullet points is because they live in a media-saturated culture like the rest of us. Almost every waking moment of our lives, we are all exposed to visuals and sounds streaming across the screens of televisions, theaters, computers, and advertising displays. But that all comes to an abrupt halt when we look at the walls in our meeting rooms and see them filled with bullet points.

We all expect an increasing standard of production quality for every type of communication, including PowerPoint presentations. Boards of directors and audiences everywhere want much more than just a "visual aid" tacked onto a classical verbal presentation. They want a sophisticated communication experience in which spoken words and visuals blend together into a seamless integrated media experience that helps everyone to understand ideas and make decisions more effectively.

To transform your PowerPoint presentations into the type of experience that audiences expect, you'll need to adapt some ideas from the world's leading experts in bullet-free communication. And to find them, you need look no farther than north of your downtown Los Angeles office building to see their symbolic home—Hollywood.

Introducing the Hollywood Approach

Hollywood films and PowerPoint presentations actually have much in common. Both use spoken words and projected visuals to communicate information, and both aspire to engage people and keep them interested throughout an entire experience. But the difference is that Hollywood somehow manages to do its job successfully without bullet points. Its secret? Hollywood films *tell stories*. PowerPoint presentations usually do not.

Hollywood has always known that a story is a powerful, effective, and efficient communication technique. No one needs special training or technology to understand a story, because it's the way humans have been communicating with one another throughout history. The structures of stories follow natural patterns that underlie the way we think and understand. Stories frame the context for communication and focus attention by making information specific and relevant to an audience. When you apply what Hollywood knows about stories to your PowerPoint presentations, you will quickly and dramatically transform your communications well beyond bullet points.

Interpreting Classical Ideas with Modern Technology

Of course, Hollywood didn't invent the idea of a story. It simply used the new technology of film to adapt the classical elements of storytelling recorded by the Greek philosopher Aristotle 2,400 years ago. It wouldn't be unusual today to walk into a Hollywood film school and hear filmmakers debating the fine points of Aristotle's classical ideas about plot, character, and three-act structure.

Just as film was a new technology that Hollywood filmmakers used to adapt Aristotle's ideas, PowerPoint is a powerful new technology that presenters can use to interpret these classical concepts. As the number of presentations dramatically increases, it is clear that all of us who use PowerPoint to communicate need to remember what Hollywood has never forgotten: *it's all about the story*. When you adapt this timeless idea to your PowerPoint presentations, you will ground your communications in a powerful technique that has worked effectively throughout human history.

Aligning Your Strategy with the Research

Before you say "Hello to Hollywood," it's important to recognize that Hollywood techniques have limitations in the context of PowerPoint presentations. Most of us go to a Hollywood movie for entertainment, but you're not giving a presentation at next week's board meeting to entertain. You'll be trying to persuade your audience to do or think something new, which will take more than razzle-dazzle. Although you do want to use sophisticated media techniques to communicate, you don't want your presentation to offer only sizzle and no substance.

Your PowerPoint approach should be informed by the latest research on how to use words and images to help people *understand* information. At the end of your presentation, you want your audience to comprehend and act on your ideas and not just remember your fancy slides or your fine performance. Fortunately, there is a body of research-based design principles that can provide you with the guidance you need as you adapt the fundamentals of the Hollywood process to PowerPoint. Many of these principles are already embedded into the process described in this book, and you can explore them in more detail in Appendix A.

Understanding the Three-Step Approach

What works for Hollywood will also work for you as you transform the Contoso presentation or any PowerPoint presentation beyond bullet points. With this book, you will adapt the process Hollywood has tested and refined through countless successful bullet-free films. This time-tested process consists of three basic steps, depicted in Figure 1-3.

To create a PowerPoint presentation without bullet points

1 Write a script to focus your ideas.

2 Storyboard your script to clarify your ideas.

3 Produce your script to engage your audience.

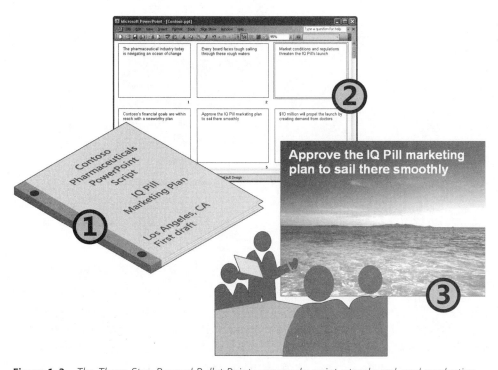

Figure 1-3 *The Three-Step Beyond Bullet Points approach: script, storyboard, and production.*

Writing a Script to Focus Your Ideas

The single most important thing you can do to dramatically improve your presentations is to have a story to tell *before* you work on your PowerPoint file. To learn how to do this effectively, you can follow Hollywood's lead.

In Hollywood, stories take a specific shape in the form of a document called a *script*. A script is much shorter and less detailed than a novel because it assumes that the visuals of a film will play a major role in telling the story. Instead of relying on long narrative descriptions, a script focuses on action and dialog. The best scripts distill stories to their bare essence and strip away anything that does not contribute to a story's singular focus.

Figure 1-4   *The concept of a Hollywood script is the inspiration for the Beyond Bullet Points Story Template.*

When a writer finishes a script, the document then becomes a powerful organizing tool that literally puts everyone on the same page. The script is the starting point for getting funding, attracting actors, and planning visuals, and it serves as a way for everyone to be clear on what everyone else is saying and doing. If you were a filmmaker and you started filming before you had a script, you would waste time and resources while you changed the plot, characters, and setting as you figured out the story along the way.

You'll take Hollywood's cue and kick off an efficient and effective process for your Contoso presentation by writing a PowerPoint script first, as shown in Figure 1-4. This step of writing a story first focuses your ideas and helps you figure out what you want to say and how you want to say it. Although writing a script adds a new step to your usual PowerPoint process, doing so will save you time and effort later.

To write a script, you need to momentarily set aside PowerPoint design issues like fonts, colors, backgrounds, and slide transitions. Although it might sound counterintuitive, when you write a script first, you actually expand your visual possibilities, because writing defines your purpose before you start designing. The more time you spend writing, the better your visuals will become. A script unlocks the undiscovered power of PowerPoint as a visual storytelling tool in ways that might surprise and delight you and your audiences.

REMEMBER Writing a script first will save you time and effort later, and improve the quality of your visuals.

When you begin writing your PowerPoint script in Chapter 2, you won't have to start with an empty page, because you'll use the Beyond Bullet Points Story Template in Microsoft Word to guide you every step of the way. The story template makes your job of writing a PowerPoint story as easy as filling in the blanks, because it includes all of the essential elements of a classical story. Just as Aristotle's ideas about story structure have shaped an endless variety of Hollywood stories, your story template includes a classical story structure that serves as the springboard for an endless variety of story possibilities for bullet-free PowerPoint presentations.

In addition to helping you tell a story, the story template helps you to figure out what you want to say and the order in which to say it. The challenge of any presentation is not to show *all* the information you have but instead to select the *right* information to present. The story template guides you through the important process of selecting only the ideas your audience needs to know and breaking them into digestible chunks that are easier for your audience to understand. All of your hard work pays off when you transform your story template into a PowerPoint storyboard.

Storyboarding Your Script to Clarify Your Ideas

With a completed script in hand, a Hollywood filmmaker usually turns to a storyboard artist to sketch selected scenes from the story to show how things will look on screen. Storyboards help teams collaborate effectively—the sketches help everyone see how the story will look so that they can plan various aspects of production such as staging, camera positioning, and lighting

You'll tap into many of these powerful benefits by adapting Hollywood's storyboarding concept to your PowerPoint presentation, as shown in Figure 1-5. You won't need to sketch anything, but will instead adapt the basic idea of treating your slides as a sequence of illustrated frames on a storyboard. When you finish focusing your ideas with the story template, you will have a solid story that sets the foundation for your spoken words and visuals. In Chapter 4, you will transform your story template into a PowerPoint storyboard as you prepare and plan your visuals in Slide Sorter view.

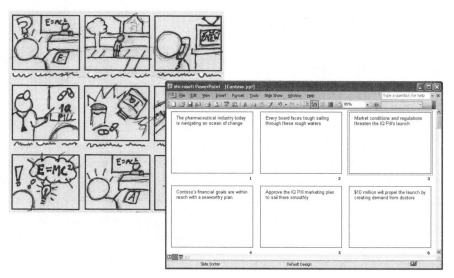

Figure 1-5   *The concept of a Hollywood storyboard is the inspiration for the Beyond Bullet Points storyboarding approach.*

In Chapter 5, you will add visuals and words to specific slides using a simple and elegant style that makes your job of turning your words into visuals much easier and faster. Don't worry if you don't have a professional designer working with you, because all the design techniques in this book are accessible to everyone.

Your storyboard will solve many of the problems with the example Contoso slides or any PowerPoint presentation because you start designing with a strong and coherent foundation in the form of a strong story. From the start, you will be able to work with your story in Slide Sorter view to review your story structure and sequence, check your pacing and flow, and use visuals to tie together

> **REMEMBER**   A storyboard sets the foundation for your spoken words and projected visuals.

the various parts of your story. This planning ensures that you continually build on and improve your strong story foundation with a single unified set of visuals and words. Developing your storyboard also increases your confidence in your topic and cultivates new and creative communication skills.

Producing Your Script to Engage Your Audience

Usually, you experience the final results of a Hollywood script on a movie screen when you buy a ticket for a new release, find a seat, and sit back and relax as the lights go down and you watch the show. But next week you are giving a live presentation to a live audience, so you'll stretch the Hollywood model into the domain of live performance, as illustrated in Figure 1-6.

Figure 1-6   *A blend of a movie and a live performance is the inspiration for the Beyond Bullet Points concept of production.*

Using the approach described in this book, you'll be well-equipped to produce a media experience that will get you the results you want anytime you give a presentation. Focusing your ideas using a story template and clarifying them using a storyboard blends your message with your media, and dramatically expands your ability to enhance your presentation with sophisticated media tools and techniques. And every step of the way, you refine your ideas and continually rehearse the way you'll present them.

Your new storyboard improves the way visuals promote meaningful communication for both you and your audience. When you project your PowerPoint slides on a large screen, they work as visual triggers that increase your confidence as a speaker. You're no longer tied to the uncomfortable task of reading text off the screen and unintentionally ignoring your audience. Instead your slides briefly signal what you'll cover and remind you about the point you want to make. While the slide is displayed, you are free to look at your audience instead of at the slide.

Because your slides are simple, they minimize the work your audience must do to figure out what you're saying. By decreasing the attention your audience would pay to complicated slides, you'll increase the attention they pay to you and your ideas. The result is an engaging multimedia experience that balances visual and verbal elements and contributes to meaningful understanding.

And even if you had a fear of public speaking in the past, you'll breathe much easier with your new PowerPoint approach. These powerful tools increase your confidence and improve the quality of everything you communicate with your spoken words and projected images. Because you're more relaxed as a speaker, you'll become more confident in improvising during your live presentation.

The three-step Beyond Bullet Points approach opens dramatic new possibilities for treating your PowerPoint screen as a canvas to promote dialog and collaboration. You'll use a classical story structure and innovative techniques to engage your audience, but there are many more things you can do to help them feel more involved. You'll explore these techniques in Chapter 7.

Getting Started

Now that you've analyzed your presentation problem, selected a strategy, and reviewed the three-step Beyond Bullet Points approach, it's time to transform your Contoso presentation.

To get started on your Contoso presentation, you need a basic project plan, so you use Microsoft Outlook to send a meeting request for review sessions with your CEO, Chris Gray. Here are the milestones for this project:

Project plan for the Contoso presentation

1. Wednesday: Meet with CEO to review script.

2. Friday: Meet with CEO to review storyboard.

3. Monday: Meet with CEO to rehearse production.

4. Wednesday: Deliver presentation at board meeting.

Now that you've defined your project milestones, you're ready to move beyond bullet points into a new world of focus, clarity, and engagement.

Chapter 2: **Setting the Stage for Your Story in Act I**

In this chapter, you will:

1. Establish the purpose of your presentation.

2. Tailor the presentation to fit your audience.

3. Learn how to grab and keep your audience's attention.

4. Make an emotional connection.

5. Give your audience a personal reason to remain interested.

When audiences such as the Contoso board of directors complain about unfocused, wordy, and dull slides, what they're really telling you is that they want the information to be easier to understand. For thousands of years, the single most effective way to simplify information has been to turn it into a story.

The basics of good storytelling have been an open secret since Aristotle described them 2,400 years ago, and today you can tap into the power of these classical ideas by applying a story structure to your PowerPoint presentations. A story can help you to focus your ideas, clarify your words and images, and produce an engaging experience for both you and your audiences. By reaching into the past and incorporating these fundamental ideas in your PowerPoint story, you'll be building on a solid foundation that ensures that your presentation is focused, clear, and engaging.

The Beyond Bullet Points Story Template

Professional Hollywood screenwriters can spend years learning their craft. Obviously, you don't have time to study Aristotle or learn the art of Hollywood screenwriting in time for the board meeting next week. You need to produce a PowerPoint presentation now.

To help get your job done quickly and efficiently, the fundamentals of classical story structure and the screenwriting process have already been adapted to your PowerPoint needs and incorporated into the Beyond Bullet Points Story Template. This template, shown in Figure 2-1, is available as a free downloadable Microsoft Office Word document at *www.sociablemedia.com*.

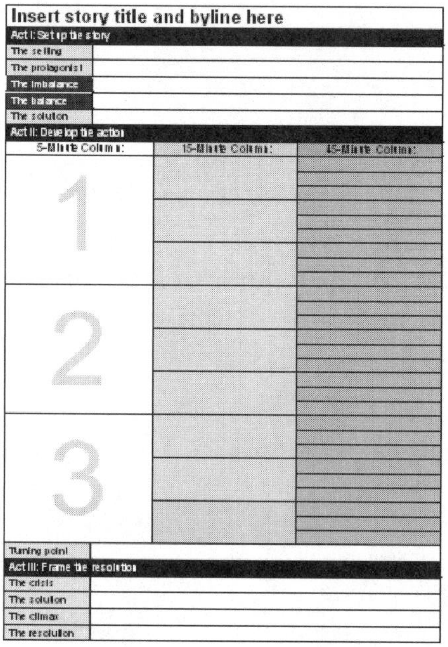

Figure 2-1 *The Beyond Bullet Points Story Template incorporates a classical story structure.*

Through the course of this book, you'll complete a story template step by step for your fictional Contoso presentation.

Before you begin entering a story in the template, prepare it by adding a title and byline.

SEE ALSO For more examples of completed story templates describing a range of other topics, visit www.sociablemedia.com

1 Download the story template file from *www.sociablemedia.com*, save it on your local computer, and open it.

2 In the top cell of the template, replace the text *Insert story title and byline here* with the title of your script—in this example, **Contoso Marketing Presentation**.

3 Type a byline for the script following the title—in this example, **by Pat Coleman**, as shown here:

Contoso Marketing Presentation by Pat Coleman	
Act I: Set up the story	
The setting	
The protagonist	
The imbalance	
The balance	
The solution	

Now that you've added a title and byline, the story template is ready for you to start writing your PowerPoint script. The template includes the three sections, or *acts*, that comprise a classical story structure and correspond to the beginning, middle, and end of your story. Each act in the template is delineated by a horizontal black bar extending across the page.

Act I begins a story by setting up all of the key story elements, including the setting, the main character, a conflict, and the desired outcome. Act II drives the story forward by picking up on the conflict in Act I and developing it through the actions and reactions of the main character in response to changing conditions. Act III ends the story by framing a climax and a decision that the main character must face to resolve the situation, revealing something about his or her character. This time-tested structure keeps your audience interested in your presentation and eager to find out what happens next.

Why a Byline Is Important

The byline of the story template is important because it names the person who is responsible for the story's successful delivery: the presenter. In many organizations, PowerPoint files will pass through many hands as they're being developed and ownership can become easily lost or unclear. The impact of these presentations diminishes because they are disconnected from the real names and faces of the people who will stand at the podium. Many people can contribute to a presentation, but no matter how many people do, only one person will ultimately make the presentation. The byline at the top of the story template makes it clear at all times the name of the person behind the slides, whose reputation and credibility are on the line.

You don't have to be an expert storyteller; the template makes structuring your story as easy as filling in the blanks. The horizontal rows in your template represent *scenes*. In these rows, you'll add text that describes what is happening at each point in your story. As you fill in the blanks, you actually will be writing the story you will present. When you've finished, you'll have a completed one-page or two-page script.

REMEMBER Act I sets up the story. Act II develops the action. Act III frames the resolution.

This built-in process ensures that you stay focused on your ideas and include all the elements that make up a good story. In addition, the template helps you to think about your ideas in a systematic way that distills your complicated ideas to their essence. This template approach will help you focus on one clear story that you can then interpret visually in a variety of ways.

Of course the purpose of your Contoso presentation next week is not only to tell an engaging story but also to persuade the board to do something specific – to approve your marketing plan. In addition to a classic story structure your template also incorporates persuasive techniques that are useful for many types of presentations in different contexts. These techniques include using Aristotle's classical concept that to persuade you need to appeal to emotion, reason, and personal credibility. Even if your intent is to simply *inform* an audience about something, you still have to *persuade* them to pay attention. Why should they listen? What's in it for them? Your story template will make sure that you persuade your audience to focus on your message.

SEE ALSO In Chapters 4, 5, and 6 you'll transform your template into a storyboard and add graphical elements to illustrate your story.

Your completed story template document becomes a useful tool that enables you to review your complete story structure on only a page or two. You'll use this document when you review your new story structure with the Contoso CEO at your Wednesday meeting. But before you start writing, you'll need to learn the three ground rules that

REMEMBER The story template structure is based on Aristotle's classical ideas about how to tell a story and persuade an audience.

apply to every statement in your story template. Like a Hollywood script, your PowerPoint script calls for a special style of writing that is concise, focused, and serves a specific purpose.

Writing Using Three Ground Rules

When you write your PowerPoint script using the story template, you focus on your ideas first because right now *it's all about the story*. After you complete your template, you'll send your Word document to PowerPoint, where each statement will fill the title area of a slide, as shown in Figure 2-2.

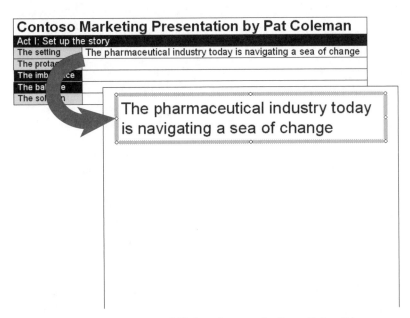

Figure 2-2 *Each statement will fill the title area of a PowerPoint slide.*

This pivotal technique of turning your story template into a set of PowerPoint slides will help you to transform your written words into the foundation of a visual story in PowerPoint. It will make your job of finding visuals easier by establishing exactly what you need to illustrate on every slide, and it will help your audience to understand your slides much faster by indicating clearly in the title area the meaning of every slide.

Because the text in your story template will fill the title area in your PowerPoint slides, your sentences will require a certain format. You achieve this format by following three important ground rules when you write.

Rule 1: Write Complete Sentences with a Subject and a Verb in Active Tense

Everything you do in your presentation from this point forward will build on the statements you write in your story template. To effectively communicate your message consistently and clearly through your entire story, your statements must be complete sentences with a subject and a verb. The verbs should be in active tense to keep your language dynamic and direct; the same principles, techniques, and rules that define good writing also define good sentences in your template.

SEE ALSO For an excellent reference guide to writing the statements of your story template clearly and concisely, see William Strunk Jr. and E. B. White, The Elements of Style (Longman, 2000).

Writing complete sentences imposes a discipline on your ideas by forcing you to turn them into coherent thoughts and remove any ambiguity. Later, when you place your statements in the title area of your slides, your audience will have no doubt about what you want to communicate because they can read it for themselves.

An additional benefit of writing complete sentences also becomes clear when you review the title areas of your slides all at one time in Slide Sorter view. You'll be able to read the complete sentences of your story across the sequence of slides—in effect allowing you to use Slide Sorter view as a storyboard to help you plan your visuals, just as a filmmaker would.

Rule 2: Use a Conversational Tone That Is Simple, Clear, and Direct

Each statement in your story template will speak directly to your audience when it fills the title area of a slide, so use a conversational tone that is simple, clear, and direct. When you write your sentences, imagine that you are addressing a few members of your audience sitting in chairs next to your desk. Because you're simply having a conversation, your voice should be relaxed and casual—not tense and formal. This conversational tone will help you to avoid jargon and will keep your sentences from getting wordy.

Three Ground Rules for Writing

Like a Hollywood script, your story template depends on a special writing style that boils down your story to its essence. Follow these three ground rules to keep your writing concise:

1 Write complete sentences with a subject and a verb in active tense.

2 Use a conversational tone that is simple, clear, and direct.

3 Constrain the length of your sentences to the limits of the template.

Later, when your audience reads your statements in the title area of your slides, the conversational tone will help them to feel more relaxed and open to your ideas.

Rule 3: Constrain the Length of Your Sentences to the Limits of the Template

When you write your sentences for Act I, constrain them to only one line that fills the width of the cell without extending to a second line. The columns in your template for Act II are narrower, so you can extend those sentences to a maximum of about two and a half lines. In Act III, you'll follow the same constraints as you did in Act I. Constraining your sentences to these limits keeps you from being wordy and ensures that your sentences will fill a maximum of two lines when you send them to the title area of your PowerPoint slides.

TIP   If you're looking for practical examples of how to write concisely, look no further than the headlines of a newspaper. When writing a headline, an editor has limited space to communicate an idea clearly, so the language tends to be clear, direct, and engaging.

It might be a challenge to keep your sentences brief, but that's part of the process of boiling down your complicated ideas to their essence. This distillation will help you to get right to the point in your presentations.

Now that you've prepared your story template and reviewed the ground rules, you're ready to start writing. Although writing is usually considered a solitary experience, you don't have to write your PowerPoint script alone. Invite the members of your team to join you in a conference room. To get started, attach a projector to your laptop computer and display your story template as a Word document on the screen, as shown in Figure 2-3.

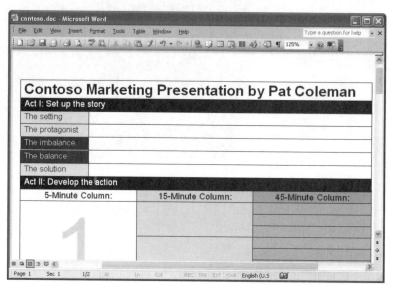

Figure 2-3   *The Contoso story template projected as a Word document.*

Act I: Setting Up Your Story

Act I is the beginning of your story. It should pull your audience out of the flow of everyday life, focus their attention, and orient them. In the story template, Act I contains five horizontal rows, each of which designates a single *scene*, as shown in Figure 2-4.

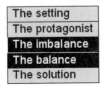

Figure 2-4   *The five scenes of Act I displayed as five rows in the story template.*

These five scenes will answer the clarifying questions that every audience silently asks every presenter: *where*, *when*, *who*, *what*, *why*, and *how*.

In Act I, you shape the answers to these questions in a creative way that awakens the imagination of your audience, connects with their emotions, and persuades them that they want to participate in your story.

Act I, Scene 1: Establishing the Setting

The first scene of Act I establishes the setting for your entire presentation. In a Hollywood film, if a scene takes place in the living room of a house in the daytime, you might first see a shot of the exterior of the house in daylight that then fades into a shot of the living room where the action will take place. This film technique is called an *establishing shot* and quickly shows the audience the *where* and *when* of a story.

To begin writing the first scene of Act I, type a statement in the row labeled *The setting* that describes the establishing shot and answers the questions your audience members are silently wondering: "*Where* are we, and *when* is it?" *Where* is not necessarily a literal geographic location but could be an abstract setting such as a profession or a general topic of discussion that establishes the context for the presentation. *When* could be an implied time, such as today, if that's obvious to the audience. For the setting of Act I, Scene 1 of the Contoso story, enter **The pharmaceutical industry today is navigating a sea of change**, as shown in Figure 2-5.

Contoso Marketing Presentation by Pat Coleman	
Act I: Set up the story	
The setting	The pharmaceutical industry today is navigating a sea of change
The protagonist	
The imbalance	
The balance	
The solution	

Figure 2-5 *Act I, Scene 1 in the story template.*

The subject of this statement, "the pharmaceutical industry," establishes the location for this presentation in this specific field of business, and "today" indicates the time frame. Now that the *where* and *when* have been established, the rest of the Scene 1 statement can say something about the setting that everyone in the room agrees is true—in this example, that the industry "is navigating a sea of change." The statement should be acceptable to everyone, because if you say something controversial or unclear, you'll quickly derail your presentation before you even get started.

This first scene is important because when your presentation begins, everyone in the audience has a different expectation. Scene 1 invites them to join you at the same location, establishes a common ground, and leaves no doubt about the context for what you are about to say.

Using the metaphor of the sea in this example communicates the idea of something big that is in constant change and also implies complexity and risk. If you carry the metaphor of the sea through other scenes you write, it becomes a *motif*, or a recurring theme, in your story. A motif is one of the most powerful techniques you can apply to your presentations. It carries your ideas all the way through your story in a coherent way, adds color and interest to your language, and makes new information easier to understand. It also makes the job of searching for graphics to add to your slides significantly easier because you can map the motif to your visuals.

> ## Act I, Scene 1
>
> Scene 1 answers the question the audience members are silently wondering: "Where are we, and when is it?"

If you use a motif, choose something that everyone in your audience can relate to, and keep it simple, clear, and easy to understand. The motif should couch and complement your ideas without becoming convoluted or a cliché or making things confusing. Consider a motif related to a personal interest you have—for example, if you love sports, you might choose your favorite sport as a motif, or if you like music, you might choose a musical theme. Choosing a motif related to your personal interests makes you more comfortable with presenting, draws out your personality and warmth, and brings your ideas to life with your natural enthusiasm.

After you add a statement for Act I, Scene 1, it's time to move to Scene 2 and add some character to the presentation.

Act I, Scene 2: Naming the Protagonist

Every story is about somebody, and that includes your PowerPoint story. The *protagonist* of your story is the main character—the person who will make a decision to do something or come to believe something by the end of the experience. According to this definition, the protagonist of every presentation is *your audience*. Because your audience acts as the main character in your story, you as the presenter become the supporting character to your audience's leading role. This means that your entire presentation is not "speaker support" but rather "audience support."

REMEMBER The *protagonist* of every presentation is your audience, and you are a supporting character. This is the crucial spin on crafting stories for live presentations.

The protagonist of a presentation could be a single person, such as a customer or client, or it could be a group, such as a committee, a team, a board, or an organization. In this presentation, the board of directors is the protagonist because they collectively will decide whether they will adopt your marketing plan.

Now that you have a star for the leading role in your presentation, write a statement for Scene 2 that affirms your audience's identity in the setting you described in Scene 1. In the row labeled *The protagonist*, type a statement that answers the question your audience is wondering: "*Who* are we in this setting?" In the Contoso example, enter **Every board faces tough sailing through these rough waters**, as shown in Figure 2-6.

Contoso Marketing Presentation by Pat Coleman	
Act I: Set up the story	
The setting	The pharmaceutical industry today is navigating a sea of change
The protagonist	Every board faces tough sailing through these rough waters
The imbalance	
The balance	
The solution	

Figure 2-6   *Act I, Scene 2 in the story template.*

The subject of this statement, "every board," subtly establishes the audience, the Contoso board of directors, as the protagonist of this story. Now that the *who* of the story is clear, the rest of the statement can simply affirm something about the

protagonist's situation that everyone in the room can agree on. In this case, everyone on the board would concur that they face "tough sailing through these rough waters." This Scene 2 statement extends the motif of the sea from Scene 1 by using the colorful phrases "tough sailing" and "rough waters."

Act I, Scene 2

Scene 2 answers the question the audience is silently wondering: *"Who* are we in this setting?"

Establishing your audience as the protagonist in your story makes your presentation personal to them. Because the audience members have a direct involvement and stake in the outcome, they will pay attention. Making your audience the protagonist also helps you to stay focused on your audience and makes sure that you tailor your presentation to their needs. This creates a positive feedback loop—when you orient your presentation around your audience, they enjoy it more, and so will you.

In the next scene, it's time to stir things up for the protagonist.

Act I, Scene 3: Describing the Imbalance

Stories are about how people respond to something that has changed in their environment. We like stories of how other people handle changes in circumstances and what their choices reveal about their characters.

When a protagonist experiences a change, an imbalance is created because things are no longer like they used to be. In screenwriting, this change is called the *inciting incident* that sets a story in motion. Scene 3 of the story template should help your audience to understand why they are there for the presentation—usually, because a change has happened that has created an imbalance.

Defining the imbalance that has brought everyone to the presentation can be easy or difficult, depending on your situation. The imbalance could be caused by a crisis brought on by an external force that has changed your organization's environment, such as a sudden economic shift or the action of a competitor. It could be the result of an internal change, such as a revised opinion or mindset, a new piece of information, a new research report, or an anecdote from the field.

On the up side, an imbalance could be brought on by an inspiration, a new idea, a discovery, or the appearance of a new opportunity that the protagonist hadn't seen before. On the down side, the imbalance could be the realization that a mistake was made, a fall from grace, the loss of market share, declining profits, or sudden drop in status. Whether positive or negative, all of these imbalances are the core reasons why people gather for presentations.

REMEMBER An inciting incident creates an imbalance that sets your story in motion.

Your Act 1, Scene 3 statement should establish the imbalance in the Contoso story. Do this by answering the question your audience is wondering: "*Why* are we here?" in the row labeled *The imbalance*. In this example, enter the statement **Market conditions and regulations threaten the IQ Pill's launch**, as shown in Figure 2-7.

SEE ALSO For more inspiration in describing your inciting incident, see "Tip 2: 10 Story Variations," later in this chapter.

Contoso Marketing Presentation by Pat Coleman	
Act I: Set up the story	
The setting	The pharmaceutical industry today is navigating a sea of change
The protagonist	Every board faces tough sailing through these rough waters
The imbalance	Market conditions and regulations threaten the IQ Pill's launch
The balance	
The solution	

Figure 2-7 *Act I, Scene 3 in the story template.*

The subject of the statement, "market conditions and regulations," describes the imbalance that starts the emotional engine of your presentation. Even though the board would probably prefer the marketing launch of the IQ Pill to be problem-free, you make it clear in Scene 3 that a smooth launch is not guaranteed because market conditions and regulations "threaten the IQ Pill's launch" like storm clouds. Using a strong and colorful word such as "threaten" conveys a sense of danger and creates an imbalance that your audience will want to resolve.

Notice that the motif of the sea continues to be simple and flexible enough to give you many creative options for the wording of your scenes. You might find in other presentations that your motif doesn't quite work as you planned. In that case, you would need to backtrack and revise the motif through the various scenes.

The inciting incident of Scene 3 defines your story and helps you to focus. You could tell a thousand stories about any particular topic; focusing on a single imbalance helps you to narrow your scope to a single story presented to a specific group of people at a particular moment in time.

> ### Act I, Scene 3
> Scene 3 answers the question your audience is silently wondering: "*Why* are we here?"

But despite the storms that might be looming on the horizon in your presentation, things will start looking better in Scene 4.

Act I, Scene 4: Aiming for Balance

No one likes to remain in a state of imbalance. When something changes, we all feel unsettled and emotionally uncomfortable until we bring the situation back into equilibrium. The same holds true for the protagonist in the Contoso story or in any presentation.

In Scene 3, you described a change for your audience that has created an imbalance. In Scene 4, they want to see how things will look when the situation is brought back into balance. To write the fourth scene of Act I, in the row labeled *The balance*, type an answer to the question your audience is wondering: "*What* do we want to see happen?" In this example, enter **Contoso's financial goals are within reach with a seaworthy plan**, as shown in Figure 2-8.

Contoso Marketing Presentation by Pat Coleman	
Act I: Set up the story	
The setting	The pharmaceutical industry today is navigating a sea of change
The protagonist	Every board faces tough sailing through these rough waters
The imbalance	Market conditions and regulations threaten the IQ Pill's launch
The balance	Contoso's financial goals are within reach with a seaworthy plan
The solution	

Figure 2-8   *Act I, Scene 4 in the story template.*

The subject of this sentence, "Contoso's financial goals," indicates what the board members want to see after they weather the threatening conditions you are describing, and you let them know that what they want is "within reach." This establishes the desired outcome that will bring the protagonist's situation back into balance. After this question is answered, you can add a phrase such as the one here—"with a seaworthy plan"—that adds a hint about what it will take to reach that balance.

In Scenes 1 through 3 of Act I, you created a picture of the board sailing through a sea of change, with challenges threatening them. Scene 4 shows them a vision of the safe destination they want to find in this

> ## Act I, Scene 4
> Scene 4 answers the question the audience is asking themselves: "*What* do we want to see happen?"

context. When they see where they want to go, they'll be fueled by their desire to get there under your expert guidance.

In the story template, the two cells that indicate Scene 3 and Scene 4 have darkly shaded backgrounds because together these two scenes form the emotional engine that will energize your audience throughout your presentation, as shown in Figure 2-9. Scenes 3 and 4 define the problem that you are there to help your audience to solve and also establish for the audience "What's in this for us?"

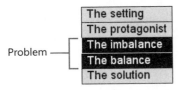

Figure 2-9   *The problem is defined in Scenes 3 and 4.*

Remember, Scene 3 puts your audience in an uncomfortable state of imbalance, and Scene 4 describes the state of balance that they want to achieve. These two scenes spark off of one another to generate the energy that drives your story forward and makes your audience eager to hear your proposed solution.

The problem described by Scenes 3 and 4 not only helps your audience engage with your presentation, but it also helps you to select and prioritize information. Of all the information available to you, how do you know which information to include? The answer is to select only information that specifically helps your audience close the gap between Scenes 3 and 4. Any other information is unnecessary for this presentation and can be set aside for another story on another day.

The problem created by Scenes 3 and 4 also forms the *purpose* of your presentation, so when you make the problem clear, you make your purpose clear. This problem is central to your entire presentation and forms the singular question that your presentation will try to answer. It creates an emotional center of gravity that focuses your story and makes it cohere across all of its separate parts.

Defining the problem for your audience is probably the hardest thing you'll do in your presentation. You and your team might go through several rounds of drafts and revisions to get Scenes 3 and 4 right, but when you do, the rest of your presentation will fall into place.

When you have a clear problem established in Scenes 3 and 4, it's time to let your audience know how you propose to solve it.

Act I, Scene 5: Recommending a Solution

In screenwriting, a *plot point* is where the action in a film suddenly turns in a particular direction and sets up the development of the next part of a story. You will create a plot point at the end of Act I by addressing the tension you created with the problem in Scenes 3 and 4. Remember, Scene 3 sets up an imbalance, and Scene 4 shows your audience what a new state of balance looks like. The fifth and final scene of Act I should propose a solution to the problem formed by the previous two scenes, as shown in Figure 2-10.

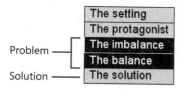

Figure 2-10   *The solution is given in Scene 5.*

Scene 5 is the reason you're the presenter—you've taken the time to figure out how the protagonist can solve the problem. To complete the fifth scene, in the row labeled *The solution*, type an answer to the question your audience would probably like to know about their desired state of balance in Scene 4: "*How* do we get there from here?" In this case, enter **Approve the IQ Pill marketing plan and we'll sail there smoothly**, as shown in Figure 2-11.

Contoso Marketing Presentation by Pat Coleman	
Act I: Set up the story	
The setting	The pharmaceutical industry today is navigating a sea of change
The protagonist	Every board faces tough sailing through these rough waters
The imbalance	Market conditions and regulations threaten the IQ Pill's launch
The balance	Contoso's financial goals are within reach with a seaworthy plan
The solution	Approve the IQ Pill marketing plan to sail there smoothly

Figure 2-11   *Act I, Scene 5 in the story template.*

In this example, you recommend that the Contoso board of directors "approve the IQ Pill marketing plan" to get to where they want to be in Scene 4, and in the process solve the problem formed by Scenes 3 and 4. In the context of a threatening sea, they see their financial goals in the distance, and they will be able to "sail there smoothly" if they follow your recommendation to approve the plan.

Scene 5 should describe what the protagonist should do or believe to solve the problem. This scene is extremely important because it is the plot point that determines what happens next as you develop the

> ## Act I, Scene 5
> Scene 5 answers the question your audience is wondering: "*How* do we get there from here?"

action in Act II. As you go through the process of writing Act II in Chapter 3, you will thoroughly develop and test your Scene 5 solution and will likely revise the wording of this statement. Your final wording is important, because Scene 5 clearly defines the measure of success for your presentation. If your audience accepts your solution by the end of your story, you'll know you succeeded.

Closing the Curtain on Act I

Now that you have five scenes, you've completed the first draft of Act I. Review your statements. They might seem simple, but they've helped you to accomplish many important tasks, such as tailoring your presentation to your audience and establishing criteria to narrow down the information you want to communicate. Consider these scenes a working draft as you complete the rest of the story template; you might need to return to them and revise them as you develop the rest of your presentation.

If you haven't already done so, take the time now to review your five scenes with your team and anyone else who needs to approve your presentation. These statements determine everything that will unfold next in your story, so it's important to get other people involved early in this writing process to make sure that you're on the right track.

REMEMBER The five scenes of Act I form the basis for the rest of the presentation, so it's important to involve your team at this stage and get any approvals you need before moving on to Act II.

It's not uncommon for an individual or a team to completely revise Act I several times until the story is exactly right for the audience. An executive team might spend a great deal of time fine-tuning Act I because, in a bigger sense, these five statements can define the way the organization understands and relates to its customers. These five simple scenes are in fact a communications strategy and are worthy of whatever resources you normally invest in developing strategic issues.

Review the tips at the end of this chapter to develop and refine your Act I statements. Here are a couple of things you can do to test and review the statements now.

Reviewing the Five Scenes

Read the five statements aloud so that you can verify that you have the tone, flow, and clarity of language that you want. Check your scenes to make sure that you answer each of the clarifying questions that every audience wants to know: *where*, *when*, *who*, *why*, *what*, and *how*. Here are the questions in their respective scenes:

> **TIP**   If you ever have to give an off-the-cuff speech, use the five scenes of Act I as the outline for your talk. This is a sure-fire way to answer your audience's clarifying questions and leave them thoroughly impressed.

- **Scene 1:** *Where* are we, and *when* is it?

- **Scene 2:** *Who* are we in this setting?

- **Scene 3:** *Why* are we here?

- **Scene 4:** *What* do we want to see happen?

- **Scene 5:** *How* do we get there from here?

When you've clearly answered these questions, you should consider how your Act I scenes appeal to your audience and help you to focus.

Appealing to Your Audience's Emotions

The members of any audience, including the Contoso board, are not purely rational beings—they are emotional too. You can avoid a strictly rational approach by using your Act I scenes to make an emotional connection with your audience and persuade them that the information is important to them. You achieve this connection by defining a few of the most important elements of a story—the setting, protagonist, inciting incident, desired future, and plot point. By tailoring each of these elements to your audience and presenting them in Act I, you make your story personal to your audience and ensure that you are off to a strong start.

> **REMEMBER**   Your Act I scenes make an emotional connection with your audience.

Focusing Your Ideas

As you saw in the original Contoso presentation slides in Chapter 1, PowerPoint presentations commonly contain large quantities of information. If the volume of information overwhelms your audience, their minds will shut down, and you won't achieve the results you want. Act I of the story template helps you to establish criteria to narrow down all the things you *could* say to only the most important things you *should* say to this audience during this presentation. When you begin writing the Act II scenes in Chapter 3, you'll find that these Act I scenes have set up your story in a way that will limit the quantity of information to only what is necessary and the quality of information to the high standards you expect.

The process of writing Act I scenes described in this chapter covers the fundamentals that apply to any presentation story and helps you to appeal to emotion and focus your ideas. Once you learn the basics, you can apply a broad range of creative resources, tools, and techniques to help you adapt this structure to your own style and circumstance.

When you're satisfied with your Act I scenes, it's time to flesh out your story in Acts II and III. Before you move on to Chapter 3, scan through the 10 tips in the following sections to find ideas that might inspire you to improve on Act I after you're comfortable with the fundamentals.

10 Tips for Enhancing Act I

The Act I structure in the story template isn't a strict formula; it's a basic platform with the potential for endless innovation and improvisation based on the specifics of your situation. Just as Hollywood can create endless film variations using this pattern, you can likewise create endless presentation variations with this tool. After you learn the fundamentals, there's plenty of room to adapt and improvise to suit your personality, audience, and situation.

If you're ready to take your presentations to the next level, here are 10 advanced tips for building on the basic structure of Act I.

Tip 1: Inspiration from the Screenwriters

Spark your creative energy by going back to the past to see the future of presentation stories. All you need to do is consult with the original expert on story structure. Start by picking up copies of Aristotle's classics *Poetics* and *Rhetoric*. For a more recent, Hollywood adaptation of Aristotle's ideas, a number of excellent books on screenwriting can help you with writing your Act I scenes, including *Story: Substance, Structure, Style and the Principles of Screenwriting,* by Robert McKee (Regan Books, 1997); *Screenplay: The Foundations of Screenwriting,* by Syd Field (Dell, 1984); and *Stealing Fire from the Gods: A Dynamic New Story Model for Writers and Filmmakers*, by James Bonnet (Michael Wiese Productions, 1999). Any of these titles can help you learn more about the key elements of the first act of every story, including settings, character development, inciting incidents, and plot points. As you read these books for inspiration, keep in mind that your PowerPoint presentation is a specific type of story in which your audience is the protagonist and you are in a supporting role. Maintaining this focus will ensure that all of your stories align with the specific needs of your PowerPoint presentations.

Tip 2: 10 Story Variations

After you've mastered the basics of the five Act I scenes, try improvising in your stories. For example, your story structure might involve changing the order of scenes in Act I. You could place the imbalance and balance scenes first as Scenes 1 and 2 and define the setting, protagonist, and solution later. You could begin with the solution scene to grab people's attention and then continue with the other scenes. At times, you might be able to delete a scene if the audience is absolutely in agreement about a situation, although it rarely hurts to clearly restate information to bring everyone to the same starting point.

Although the classical story structure of Act I is the foundation for limitless story variations, there is a more limited set of story types that can help you to frame your own stories. In his book *Moving Mountains* (Crowell-Collier Press, 1989), Henry M. Boettinger describes a dozen story types, summarized below, that describe various situations that people in organizations might face. Many of these story types can help you to refine the imbalance/balance dynamic you set up in Act I, Scenes 3 and 4.

- **Historical narrative:** "We have a history that makes us proud, and we want to apply our high standards to the current situation."

- **Crisis:** "We have to respond to the danger facing us."

- **Disappointment:** "We made a decision based on the best information we had available, but now we know it wasn't the right decision, so we have to try something else."

- **Opportunity:** "We know something now that we didn't know before, which presents us with a new possibility if we act."

- **Crossroads:** "We've been doing fine on the path that we're on, but now we have a new choice and we have to decide which path to take."

- **Challenge:** "Someone else has achieved something amazing—do we have it in us to do the same?"

- **Blowing the whistle:** "Although it appears everything is going fine, we have a serious problem we need to fix."

- **Adventure:** "We know that trying something new is a risk, but it's better to take a risk than to stay in a rut."

- **Response to an order:** "We've been told we have to do this, so we're here to figure out how to make it happen."

- **Revolution:** "We're on a path to disaster if we don't radically change what we're doing today."

- **Evolution:** "If we don't keep up with the latest, we'll fall behind."

- **The Great Dream:** "If we can only see our possibility, we can make it our reality."

No matter what type of story you have, read through these story types when you start writing your Act I statements to see whether one of them can help to you find the words you're looking for.

Tip 3: Your Act I Screen Test

In Hollywood, a *screen test* puts actors in front of a camera to test how they will do on screen. In a PowerPoint presentation, your first screen test is for your Act I scenes, and your first audience is the members of your team.

It's important to include other people at this stage of your presentation so that you can get early feedback and fresh perspectives. If you're working on a small or an informal presentation, ask a colleague or your boss to look over your Act I scenes. If the presentation is for a team, a division, or an organization, call a meeting and project the statements on a screen so that your team can review them and verify that you're on the right track.

Creating a PowerPoint presentation can be a group activity from the start, helping you to tap into the best thinking your organization can offer. Because you're working only with your written statements, you and your team can focus exclusively on the ideas at hand and not be distracted by visuals at this critical stage in the story process.

Once you get the hang of writing an Act I with your group, try applying these techniques to other communications scenarios beyond your PowerPoint presentations. Crafting Act I of a presentation is a problem-solving framework that can also help a group to clarify strategy, develop marketing messages, create project plans, and resolve other challenges. Sharing your Act I scenes with a team is also a great way to kick off a project or orient someone new to a team. By reviewing the five scenes of Act I and the clarifying questions, team members can learn the situation quickly and efficiently.

Tip 4: Multiple Stories, Multiple Templates

When it comes to presentations, one size might not fit all.

The beauty of your Act I scenes is that they are finely tailored and tuned to solve the specific problem of a specific audience. But what if your audience has more than one problem? What if you give the same presentation to different audiences that have different problems to solve? In the Contoso example presentation, you might need to present the marketing plan to different audiences, including the board, your advertising agency, and your sales team. In each instance, the presentation will have a different focus and will need a different version of Act I. If you don't tailor your presentations to your audiences, you won't connect with them.

One way to plan for these different situations is to create several versions of Act I, each of which is tailored to a specific audience. Create a copy of the Word document that contains the five Act I scenes from your current story template. In the new document, revise Scenes 3 and 4, which describe the central problem that your new audience faces. When you change these scenes to reflect a new problem, you might find that you need to revise Scenes 1 and 2 if a different set of circumstances led to this problem. And you most likely will also need to revise Scene 5 because the solution for the new problem will probably be different from the solution to the previous problem. By creating separate versions of Act I, you can choose the most appropriate version for your next audience.

This multiple-version approach can also be used if you find that you have more stories to tell in addition to the one you're working on. If you sense another story emerging, open up a new story template, and keep it open while you're working on your current presentation, adding statements to your second story as you go. As you develop your second presentation in parallel to the first, you might find that you're able to refine both versions at the same time.

Tip 5: Visualize Your Audience

The more clearly you know your audience, the clearer your communications will become.

When you start writing your Act I scenes, take some time with your team to visualize everything that you know about your specific audience. To do this, open a blank PowerPoint presentation, create a blank slide, and insert a picture of a specific audience member or just type a specific name on the screen. If you're speaking to a large audience, consider the slide a composite of the average audience member.

Ask your group questions like these:

- What do we know about this person?

- What have we heard about his personality type?

- How does she make decisions?

- What can we learn from a Web search about his thinking process?

- What can we learn from our social network about how she works with other people?

- How do we effectively fashion an experience that aligns with his interests and personality type and not ours?

Type the information on the slide as your group gives feedback so that everyone has all the information captured on a PowerPoint slide. When you do this, you tap into the collective thinking of your group to better understand your audience. And you think more deeply about your audience and your purpose, which will significantly improve the quality of your statements.

Tip 6: What Problem Is Your Audience Facing?

To accurately define the problem your audience is facing, try putting yourself in the place of the audience.

Your Act I scenes identify a problem that your audience faces and a solution that you propose. But it's not always easy to figure out the problem so that you can be sure you have the right solution. The visualization exercise described in Tip 5 can help you to see into the mindset of your audience so that you'll be in a better position to write the appropriate scenes for them.

Another technique is role playing. When you review the rough draft of your Act I scenes, ask a member of the group to play the role of a decision-maker or representative member of your audience. She can review the material you gathered from the previous profiling exercise to help her to get into character.

Request that this person be a devil's advocate during your review session, continually asking questions such as these:

- What's in this for me?

- Why do you think this is important to me?

- Why should I care?

When you hear this critical voice during your review, you'll be able to test your scenes to make sure that you're hitting the mark. It's better to hear the questions from a fictional audience than to have them pop up unexpectedly during your actual presentation.

Once you've identified your audience's problem, don't be surprised if your presentation holds tightly together and your ideas start to emerge into clear meaning.

Tip 7: Strategic Collage

If you have a high-stakes presentation to make, you might need to invest extra effort to get to know your audience in advance. One way to get to know them is to spend a day in their shoes—at least symbolically. Open up a new PowerPoint file and then create six blank slides. On each of these slides, type one of the clarifying questions: **Where? When? Who? What? Why?** and **How?**

Use a digital camera to take pictures of the objects your audience uses every day or of the environments where they live and work and the people they might see. Your visuals should represent whatever data you have about your audience, whether it's market research, demographics, or focus group information. Use the Microsoft Office Online Clip Art and Media Gallery to download free images. Or go through your organization's photo libraries to find licensed photographs and clip art that you can use to show the buildings in which these people work, the products they use, and the places they visit. You can use a digital scanner to insert pictures of documents, a pen tablet to make sketches, a video camera to insert video clips, and a microphone to collect sound.

When you've collected these multimedia elements, arrange them on each of the six PowerPoint slides to create six collages. Size the different elements according to how important you think each is to your audience—for example, if mobility is most important, make the picture of a car larger than less important elements.

Present the file to your team as you discuss what it's like to spend a day in your audience's shoes in the context of these six slides. Then open your story template and start working on Act I. Discuss with your team how well the statements match the collages, and then edit the statements to provide a good fit. The better your Act I story matches the reality of your audience's lives, the better your presentation.

Tip 8: The Story of Advertising

Some of the most powerful examples of Act I story structure pass right before your eyes every day. If you look for them, you'll find an endless stream of ideas for your presentations. These stories are all around us—in the form of advertising.

Advertisers are well aware of Aristotle's ideas and techniques of storytelling and persuasion, because at its essence, every advertisement is a persuasive story. Whether you look up at a billboard, open a magazine, or watch television, you're seeing a mini-story built on the fundamentals of persuasion. Each advertisement has a singular goal in mind: to persuade you to do something—usually, to buy a product.

To persuade you, an advertiser will use the most current and sophisticated blend of multimedia possible. But beneath the media mix are the same classical story elements you've been working with in Act I of the story template: the clarifying questions *where*, *when*, *who*, *what*, *why*, and *how*. As in a PowerPoint presentation, the protagonist of an advertisement is usually the audience—in this case, you—because the advertiser's goal is to persuade you to buy or think something new.

So if you're watching a commercial for a laundry detergent, you can compare the questions your audience silently asks of your five Act I scenes to what you see on TV, something like this:

- *Where* are we, and *when* is it? (I'm at home, and it's the afternoon.)

- *Who* are we in this setting? (I'm a person getting ready to go out for the evening.)

- *Why* are we here? (I dropped spaghetti on my favorite shirt.)

- *What* do we want? (I want to impress my date tonight by looking my best.)

- *How* do we get there from here? (If I buy Product X laundry detergent, my shirt will be clean in time for my date.)

There's usually a one-to-one correspondence between your Act I questions and most advertisements because both have the same intent: to make an emotional connection and to persuade. And both creatively interpret the fundamentals of story structure to get the job done. The next time you notice an advertisement, observe the structure that gives it form. Sometimes the story elements might be implied or communicated using a photo, sound, or movement instead of words, but they will usually all be there.

As you begin to see this common persuasive story structure in advertising, you'll be more aware of the range of storytelling approaches, and you'll be able to apply these techniques to your own Act I scenes.

Tip 9: Persuasive Education

Educators and trainers are in the same boat as the rest of us when it comes to the challenges of communicating today. They also are impacted by the expectations of audiences who now are fluent in the visual language of Hollywood and expect the same level of media sophistication in the classroom.

For example, a university professor who's struggling to find a way to make his architecture course more interesting and engaging is struck by the fact that every one of the architects he'll discuss also struggled with change—economic change, social change, demographic change, and technological change. So he decides to adopt a classical persuasive technique and chooses the singular topic of change as the key theme of his course. The persuasive story in Act I goes like this:

- *Where* are we, and when is it? (Our culture today is undergoing seismic change.)

- *Who* are we in this setting? (Architects stand at the epicenter of economic change, social change, and technological change.)

- *Why* are we here? (When you graduate and enter your profession, you are in most danger of instability.)

- *What* do we want? (You need to find the professional grounding to anchor you, no matter what changes occur.)

- *How* do we get there from here? (Learn these techniques to ensure that you keep a firm footing.)

This persuasive Act I structure provides an elegant framework for the entire course. It gives students a way to understand the single theme and follow it through the various events in the complicated history of architecture. And the dramatic and persuasive elements give students a way to relate personally to the material.

Finding a defining structure like this is not always easy, but it can make the difference between a boring lecture and an engaging presentation. Try applying the persuasive model the next time you teach or inform, and see whether you can make things more interesting for both yourself and your audience.

Tip 10: Get the Writing Right

Beyond the nuts and bolts of writing down the words, consider ways you can apply literary techniques to convey clear meaning across your scenes. Act I is so brief and elegant that you are actually telling a rich but concise story in only five sentences. Using a motif is one powerful technique; see whether you can pick up other techniques from professional writers whose work you admire.

Writers such as poets are extremely good at communicating a great deal of information in a limited number of words. Pick up a book of poetry and pay attention to how the author uses words, metaphor, and pacing. Scan through the text in a range of newspapers, and consider how the writers manage to tell a complicated story in only a brief article. Listen to people speak, and try adapting the direct and clear phrases you hear to the words of your Act I statements. If you have good writers on your team, ask them to help write your Act I statements, and if you have the resources, hire a professional writer to help. The success of your entire presentation rests on the language you use for Act I, and any amount of time and resources you can invest in improving that language will be well spent.

And you can put that in writing.

Chapter 3: Fleshing Out Your Story in Acts II and III

In this chapter, you will:

1. Decide what you want to say and the order in which to say it.

2. Boil down a complicated idea to three main points.

3. Support your ideas with reason.

4. Eliminate unnecessary information.

5. Increase your own confidence in your topic.

Long ago, Aristotle said that a well-constructed story should have a beginning, a middle, and an end; so should every Microsoft Office PowerPoint presentation. Your PowerPoint script already has a strong beginning in the form of the Act I scenes you wrote in the Beyond Bullet Points Story Template in Chapter 2. The five scenes in Act I set the stage for your story by orienting your audience, making an emotional connection, and sparking the dynamic energy that drives your story forward. Now you'll build on this strong beginning by fleshing out your story with a middle in Act II and an end in Act III.

Introducing Acts II and III

Act I appeals primarily to emotion; it makes your story personal and relevant to your audience. Act II will appeal to reason as you develop the action of your story, and Act III will blend emotion and reason together as you frame your resolution.

Appealing to Reason in Act II

Once you've made an emotional connection with your audience in Act I, they will be ready to hear your appeal to reason in Act II. Act II is where the intellectual rubber meets the road and you deliver the reasons why people should accept the solution you proposed at the end of Act I. This is the "action" of your story that people really came to your presentation to see. But the action does not take place on a Hollywood set; instead, the action takes place in the clear and compelling world of ideas.

Your goal in Act II is to present your ideas in a way that makes sense to your audience. In preparing any presentation, you might find it difficult to determine what information is most important and the order in which to present that information to make it most convincing. Aristotle's ideas can help here too—in addition to describing ways to structure a story, he also explained how people use reason to make sense of information.

You'll apply classical techniques of reasoning as you complete Act II of your story template, boiling down your ideas into three main points and corroborating each of these points in a reasoned sequence of supporting points. This process will validate, sort, and prioritize your ideas in an order that aligns with the natural way people think. It also provides a dramatic structure for your ideas that keeps your audience interested. When you've completed this process at the end of Act II, you'll write a scene that transitions your presentation into Act III.

Appealing to Emotion and Reason in Act III

If Act I of your story template appeals primarily to emotion and Act II appeals primarily to reason, Act III brings the two preceding acts together to create a compelling end to your story. Act III resolves the set of dynamics that you set in motion in Act I and carried through the entire presentation. Your audience will be anticipating closure, and your story won't disappoint them.

Act III completes your story template, which is the foundation for your focused, clear, and engaging presentation next week. It gives you the structure you need to have in place when you begin turning the words of your script into the visuals of your storyboard. But before you get to that point, it's time to develop the action of your story in Act II.

Act II: Developing the Action

To recap your story so far: your Act I scenes define the establishing shot, the main character, the inciting incident, and the desired balance. The final scene of Act I, the solution, grabs the story and turns it in a specific direction. In this scene, you take a stand and recommend what your audience should do to solve their problem. Act II begins from this pivot point.

Centering on the Solution

Because you make your audience's problem clear in Act I, they are now paying close attention to find out how they can solve this problem. The final scene of Act I gets right to the heart of your audience's immediate concern by directly stating what they should do about the situation. In your Contoso presentation, your proposed solution in Act I, Scene 5 is to "Approve the IQ Pill marketing plan to sail there smoothly," as shown in Figure 3-1.

| The solution | Approve the IQ Pill marketing plan to sail there smoothly |

Figure 3-1   *The solution statement from Act I, Scene 5.*

Now that your audience knows your recommended solution, they're eager to hear why and how your solution is a good idea, which is what you'll explain next. Focusing exclusively on explaining your solution in Act II gives you the criteria you need to reduce the amount of information in your presentation. You'll include only information that supports your reasons for recommending the solution and exclude everything else.

SEE ALSO   As you work on Act II, refer to the completed story templates available at www.sociablemedia.com These templates include a range of Act II examples from different types of presentations.

Choosing from Three Levels of Detail

Act II in the story template contains three columns, labeled *5-Minute Column*, *15-Minute Column*, and *45-Minute Column* as shown in Figure 3-2. Each column contains a greater level of detail about your solution statement. In the 5-Minute Column, which contains only three cells, you state the three main reasons your audience should accept your solution. You must complete at least these three cells to make the story template useful. The 15-Minute Column contains an additional level of detail about the three 5-Minute Column statements, and the 45-Minute Column contains the next level of detail about the 15-Minute Column statements.

For any presentation, you can choose to complete the columns that correspond to the level of detail and length of presentation you want. The entire story template, including all three columns in Act II, contains 49 cells, each of which contains a single statement. If you spend about one minute per statement, you have enough material for a 45-minute presentation. If you skip the 45-Minute Column, you end up with a total of 22 statements in your story template; if you spend about 40 seconds on each, you have enough material for a 15-minute presentation. If you skip the 15- and 45-minute columns, you have 12 statements; at a pace of about 25 seconds each, you have a 5-minute presentation.

In this chapter, every cell in the Contoso example contains a statement so that you can see how the entire process works.

To set Act II in motion, reread your solution from Act I, Scene 5, and then ask yourself the main reasons *why* your audience should accept it or *how* they should implement it.

SEE ALSO It's always a good idea to limit your ideas to groups of three, as described in "Tip 1: The Power of Three," later in this chapter. But if you need to expand your groupings to four, you can use the expanded template version that's described in "Tip 2: Making Room for Four."

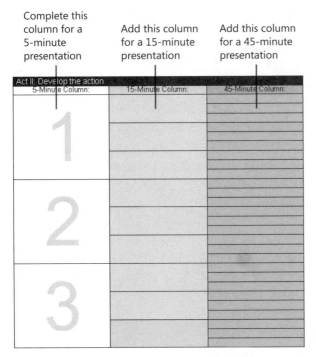

Complete this column for a 5-minute presentation

Add this column for a 15-minute presentation

Add this column for a 45-minute presentation

Figure 3-2 *Act II of the story template, showing options for presentation length based on columns of supporting detail.*

Specifying Three Main Supporting Points

Your first challenge in Act II is to boil down to three main points the many reasons why your audience should accept your recommended solution or the main steps that describe how they should implement it.

To begin filling in Act II in the story template, position your cursor to the right of the *5-Minute Column* heading. If the solution you recommend at the end of Act I is for your audience to do something, they will want to know *why* they should do it. If your solution is to follow a set of steps, they will want to know *how*. Choose the question that best describes what your audience will want to know next about your solution, and type the question to the right of the *5-Minute Column* heading—in this case, **Why?**—as shown in Figure 3-3.

The solution	Approve the IQ Pill marketing plan to sail there smoothly	
Act II: Develop the action		
5-Minute Column: Why?	15-Minute Column:	45-Minute Column:

Figure 3-3   *The 5-Minute Column indicates the question Why?*

Your 5-Minute Column heading now indicates the question that your audience is wondering about your solution—in this case, *"Why* should we approve the IQ Pill marketing plan?" You'll answer their question by explaining the three main reasons why they should approve the plan. Follow the three ground rules described in the section "Writing Using Three Ground Rules," in Chapter 2, to write out your statements in each of the three cells of the 5-Minute Column, prioritizing them in descending order of importance. Limit your sentences to a maximum of about two and a half lines, as shown in Figure 3-4.

The solution	Approve the IQ Pill marketing plan to sail there smoothly	
Act II: Develop the action		
5-Minute Column: Why?	15-Minute Column:	45-Minute Column:
$10 million will propel the launch by creating demand from doctors		
$50 million will smooth the way with demand from consumers		
The plan will navigate through all regulatory requirements		

Figure 3-4   *Act II, with the 5-Minute Column cells completed.*

In this example, the three main points continue the motif of the sea and sailing that was established in Act I. In the first main point, you explain that a $10 million investment will "propel the launch" by creating demand for the IQ Pill from doctors. In the second main point, you state that another $50 million investment will "smooth the way" for demand for the IQ Pill from consumers; and in the last main point, you state that the plan will "navigate" through all of the regulatory requirements necessary for marketing the IQ Pill. Continuing your motif from Act I into Act II gives your audience a sense of coherence and focus as you develop the details of the information to come.

Your three main points might come easily if you've been thinking about these issues for a long time and you can simply write them down. Or they might take some work because you're still figuring them out and you need to cluster together related ideas in a single main idea. If you're at a loss for words, ask someone to read the 5-Minute Column question out loud to you. Speak your answers out loud as you formulate them, and then type them in the 5-Minute Column. If you're still not sure of your answers, draft a placeholder set of three main points so that you have a place to start.

SEE ALSO For more ideas about how to boil down your ideas to their essence, see "Tip 4: Grow Clarity Using a Logic Tree" and "Tip 5: Build an Outline in a Brainstorm," later in this chapter.

When you've entered your three main points in the 5-Minute Column, test them by filling in the blanks in this sentence:

> The three main reasons *(insert protagonist from Act I)* should *(insert solution from Act I)* are: *(insert main point 1)*, *(insert main point 2)*, and *(insert main point 3)*.

In the Contoso presentation example, the completed sentence reads:

> The three main reasons *the Contoso board* should *approve the IQ Pill marketing plan* are: *$10 million will propel the launch by creating demand from doctors*, *$50 million will smooth the way with demand from consumers*, and *the plan will navigate through all regulatory requirements*.

For this sentence to sound right, each main point should be written in a similar form and should contain a similar type of information.

The 5-Minute Column Test

Test the three 5-minute Column points by filling in the blanks in this sentence:

> The three main reasons *(insert protagonist from Act I)* should *(insert solution from Act I)* are: *(insert main point 1)*, *(insert main point 2)*, and *(insert main point 3)*.

As you test your three main points, you might find that the solution isn't exactly what you intended and you need to go back and rework Act I or just revise the wording of the solution. Or you might need to revise your three main points to make sure that they each support the solution in a way that makes your test sentence sound right. You'll probably need to do a couple of rounds of testing and revising before you're satisfied with your results and are ready to move on to the next step.

When you've entered your three main points in the 5-Minute Column of your story template, you can start building the three scenes of Act II.

Act II, Scene 1: Supporting the First Main Point

The Act II scenes in the story template are structured somewhat differently from the scenes in Act I. To use a food metaphor, Act I guides your audience into a restaurant, seats them at your table, determines that they're hungry, and takes their order. Diners usually want this sequence of events to happen in the shortest possible time period—in this case, the five brief scenes of Act I. Act II presents your audience with a three-course meal, which is the reason they came to the restaurant (as well as the company, of course). People usually want this dining experience to happen at a leisurely pace so that they can enjoy their food and digest properly—like the three longer scenes they will savor in Act II.

Each Act II scene in your story template is represented by a horizontal row of cells that begins with each 5-Minute Column main point and extends to the right to include all of the adjacent cells in Columns 2 and 3, as shown in Figure 3-5.

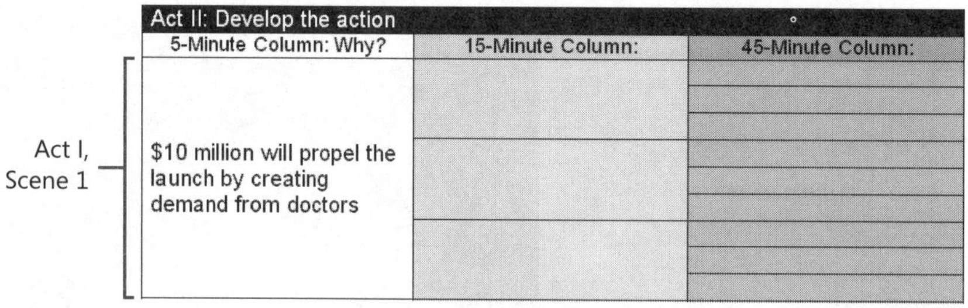

Figure 3-5 *Act II, Scene 1 extends horizontally from left to right in the story template.*

As in this example, the main point in the 5-Minute Column anchors each Act II scene by maintaining a singular focus horizontally across all three columns. The 15-and 45-minute columns will flesh out the main idea in increasing detail as you enter the statements of your scene from left to right, top to bottom.

To start writing the rest of Act II, Scene 1, position your cursor to the right of the *15-Minute Column* heading and type the question (either *why* or *how*) that your audience will want to know next about your three main ideas in the 5-Minute Column—in this case, **How?** Reread your main point in the 5-Minute Column, and ask yourself *how* this is true—in this case, "*How* will $10 million propel the launch by creating demand from doctors?" As you did in the 5-Minute Column, you should type your three answers in descending order of importance in the 15-Minute Column. When you enter your first reason in the top cell of the 15-Minute Column, your story template should look similar to Figure 3-6.

The solution	Approve the IQ Pill marketing plan to sail there smoothly	
Act II: Develop the action		
5-Minute Column: Why?	15-Minute Column: How?	45-Minute Column:
$10 million will propel the launch by creating demand from doctors	$5 million spent on ads will increase medical awareness	

Figure 3-6   *Act II, Scene 1, with the top cell of the 15-Minute Column completed.*

Enter your second answer in the cell below, and the third answer in the cell below that. Your 15-Minute Column answers should offer more detailed support for your main point in the 5-Minute Column and cite specific evidence. Your evidence might be findings from research, case studies, financial analysis, or anecdotes.

Test the three answers in the 15-Minute Column by filling in the blanks in this sentence:

> The three main reasons *(insert the 5-Minute Column point)* are:
> *(insert 15-Minute Column, answer 1)*, *(insert 15-Minute Column, answer 2)*,
> and *(insert 15-Minute Column, answer 3)*.

In this example, the test sentence reads:

> The three main reasons *$10 million will propel the launch by creating demand from doctors* are: *$5 million spent on ads will increase medical awareness*, *$3 million spent on sales calls will increase the sampling rate*, and *$2 million spent on conferences will increase visibility*.

As in your earlier test sentence, for this sentence to sound right, each answer should be written in a similar way and should contain a similar type of information. You can apply this test visually by reading the test sentence from left to right, as shown in Figure 3-7.

The solution	Approve the IQ Pill marketing plan to sail there smoothly	
Act II: Develop the action		
5-Minute Column: Why?	15-Minute Column: How?	45-Minute Column:
$10 million will propel the launch by creating demand from doctors	$5 million spent on ads will increase medical awareness	
	$3 million spent on sales calls will increase the sampling rate	
	$2 million spent on conferences will increase visibility	

Figure 3-7 *Testing the three statements in the 15-Minute Column to make sure that they support the main point in the 5-Minute Column.*

Now fill in the 45-Minute Column using the same techniques you used for the 15-Minute Column. Position your cursor to the right of the *45-Minute Column* heading, and type the question (*why* or *how*) your audience will want to know next about your 15-Minute Column statements—in this case, **Why?** The questions you choose for your column headings will vary according to your topic, and sometimes they might all be *why*, *how*, or combinations of the two. Now read each statement in the 15-Minute Column and ask why or how that statement is true. In the Contoso example, you'll be asking the question *why*, as in: "*Why* will $5 million spent on ads increase medical community awareness?"

The 15-Minute Column Test

Test the three 15-Minute Column points by filling in the blanks in this sentence:

The three main reasons *(insert 5-Minute Column point)* are: *(insert 15-Minute Column, answer 1)*, *(insert 15-Minute Column, answer 2)*, and *(insert 15-Minute Column, answer 3)*.

Position your cursor in the top cell of the 45-Minute Column, and type your three answers in descending order of importance. As you enter the answers in the 45-Minute Column, the cells will expand to hold your text. Keep your statements limited to about two and a half lines, as you did in the other two columns.

The answers you enter in the 45-Minute Column should offer more detailed support for the 15-Minute Column statement and cite specific evidence that backs it up. After you've entered three answers in the 15-Minute Column, test them by filling in the blanks in this sentence:

> The three main reasons *(insert 15-Minute Column statement)* are: *(insert 45-Minute Column, answer 1), (insert 45-Minute Column, answer 2),* and *(insert 45-Minute Column, answer 3).*

In this example, the test sentence would read:

> The three main reasons *$5 million spent on ads will increase medical awareness* are: *similar spending levels helped us to reach our targets in the past, industry averages validate the projected results,* and *ad agency figures predict that ad responses will remain stable.*

You can apply this test visually by reading the test sentence from left to right, as shown in Figure 3-8.

The solution	Approve the IQ Pill marketing plan to sail there smoothly	
Act II: Develop the action		
5-Minute Column: Why?	15-Minute Column: How?	45-Minute Column: Why?
$10 million will propel the launch by creating demand from doctors	$5 million spent on ads will increase medical awareness	Similar spending levels helped us to reach our targets in the past
		Industry averages validate the projected results
		Ad agency figures predict that ad responses will remain stable
	$3 million spent on sales calls will increase the sampling rate	
	$2 million spent on conferences will increase visibility	

Figure 3-8   *Testing the three statements in the 45-Minute Column to make sure that they support the point in the 15-Minute Column.*

After you test your *45-Minute Column* answers, go to the second statement in the 15-Minute Column and repeat this process for its corresponding *45-Minute Column* answers. Then go to the third statement in the 15-Minute Column and repeat the process for its *45-Minute Column* answers. When you've finished, you will have completed Act II, Scene 1 of your story template, as shown in Figure 3-9.

The 45-Minute Column Test

Test the three 45-Minute Column points by filling in the blanks in this sentence:

The three main reasons *(insert 15-Minute Column statement)* are: *(insert 45-Minute Column, answer 1)*, *(insert 45-Minute Column, answer 2)*, and *(insert 45-Minute Column, answer 3)*.

The solution	Approve the IQ Pill marketing plan to sail there smoothly	
Act II: Develop the action		
5-Minute Column: Why?	15-Minute Column: How?	45-Minute Column: Why?
$10 million will propel the launch by creating demand from doctors	$5 million spent on ads will increase medical awareness	Similar spending levels helped us to reach our targets in the past
		Industry averages validate the projected results
		Ad agency figures predict that ad responses will remain stable
	$3 million spent on sales calls will increase the sampling rate	Our current program resulted in a 20 percent increase in sampling
		The sales call program for Company X has been performing well
		Based on comparable pills, we can expect to meet our goals
	$2 million spent on conferences will increase visibility	At other conferences, we measured a 24 percent increase in visibility
		The schedule ensures that top decision makers will attend
		Our sales reps report good results from previous sponsorships

Figure 3-9   *Act II, Scene 1, with all cells completed.*

Now that you've finished Scene 1, it's time to move on to Scenes 2 and 3.

Act II, Scenes 2 and 3: Repeating the Process

Apply the same process to both Scenes 2 and 3. Continue to check your reasoning with test sentences at each level, and revise your story template statements as needed to keep the test sentences clear and consistent.

Act II of the story template is structured using groups of three ideas to make your ideas easier for your audience to understand, but you might find that you don't have exactly three supporting points to make at any level in the template. If you want to make only two points, simply leave the third cell blank. If you need to create four main points, see "Tip 2: Making Room for Four," later in this chapter. If you have more than four main points, you'll need to find a way to reduce that number, either by reworking your ideas or by merging several ideas into one main point.

When you complete the three scenes of Act II, your story template will likely extend across more than one page. In the completed Act II section of the Contoso story template, shown in Figure 3-10, the *45-Minute Column* statements have been abbreviated so that you can see the three scenes on a single page.

Figure 3-10 *Act II, with all three scenes completed.*

As you can see when you review your completed Act II scenes, you've done an impressive job of laying out the case for your Act I solution. You make your case with three main points, each of which is corroborated by a second and then a third level of supporting points.

Each idea you introduce in the presentation will prompt your audience to wonder "*Why* or *how* is this true?" Because each column in your story template is set up to answer either the question *why* or *how*, you can provide immediate answers. In story terms, this creates a steady dynamic of action/reaction—one column is an "action," and the next column is a "reaction" to it. This dynamic structure in Act II helps you to examine all of the possible directions for your story before you move on to Act III. It also helps you to align your information with the way people naturally think and reason, making your story more interesting and engaging.

When you've finished scenes 2 and 3, you'll turn your story in a new direction in the final scene of Act II.

Act II, Scene 4: Creating the Turning Point

The last scene of Act I turned your story in the particular direction of Act II, and now in the last scene of Act II, you need to turn your story in the direction of Act III. To help you to figure out what to say, take a moment to review your Act I scenes again, shown in Figure 3-11.

Contoso Marketing Presentation by Pat Coleman	
Act I: Set up the story	
The setting	The pharmaceutical industry today is navigating a sea of change
The protagonist	Every board faces tough sailing through these rough waters
The imbalance	Market conditions and regulations threaten the IQ Pill's launch
The balance	Contoso's financial goals are within reach with a seaworthy plan
The solution	Approve the IQ Pill marketing plan to sail there smoothly

Figure 3-11 *Act I of the Contoso story template.*

Act I, Scene 4, "The balance," defines where your audience wants to be instead of the imbalanced state you established in Scene 3. Here at the turning point in Act II, Scene 4, you should remind your audience of this desired balance. To do this, ask a question that refers to the balance they're seeking, as shown in Figure 3-12.

Turning point	Will Contoso be able to make the journey to good results?

Figure 3-12 *Act II, Scene 4 of the Contoso presentation.*

The phrase "make the journey to good results" alludes to the financial goals that the Contoso board wants to reach in Act I, Scene 4. Phrasing this as a question indicates that the situation is still unresolved, and rekindles the emotional connection you made earlier with your audience.

This turning point signals that Act II has concluded and that you're about to enter the final phase of tying everything together.

Now it's time to resolve your story conflicts in Act III.

Act III: Framing the Resolution

To recap your story up to now: Act I sets up a problem that your audience faces and then proposes a solution. Act II explains the reasons why your recommendation is a good idea and ends with a pivotal scene in which you reconfirm what your audience wants. In Act III, you'll tie everything together and set the stage for your audience to resolve the situation. Keep in mind that your audience is the protagonist of your story and that *they* need to resolve your presentation by deciding whether they will accept your recommended solution. You'll set the stage for your audience's resolution with the four scenes of Act III.

Act III, Scene 1: Restating the Crisis

The *crisis* of a story is when things reach a boiling point. You already put the pot on the stove and turned up the heat in Act I, Scenes 3 and 4, when you defined the central problem of the presentation. In those key scenes, you answer two important questions your audience is asking themselves, "*Why* are we here?" and "*What* do we want to see happen?" Now position your cursor in the top cell of Act III, Scene 1, and summarize the answer to these two questions in a single statement, as shown in Figure 3-13.

Act III: Frame the resolution	
The crisis	Market conditions and regulations threaten a successful trip
The solution	
The climax	
The resolution	

Figure 3-13   *Act III, Scene 1 of the Contoso presentation.*

This example uses the wording "market conditions and regulations" from Act I, Scene 3 and "successful trip" from Act I, Scene 4. The word "trip" connects back to the single motif of the sea voyage, bringing it all the way through Acts I, II, and III. By summarizing the core problem from Act I here, Act III, Scene 1 brings the crisis of the presentation sailing back into your audience's consciousness.

Next it's time to tell them something they already know.

Act III, Scene 2: Recommending the Solution

In the next scene, repeat the solution exactly as it appeared in Act I. To do that, in the next cell type the same statement you used in Act I, Scene 5, as shown in Figure 3-14.

Act III: Frame the resolution	
The crisis	Market conditions and regulations threaten a successful trip
The solution	Approve the IQ Pill marketing plan to sail there smoothly
The climax	
The resolution	

Figure 3-14   *Act III, Scene 2, which restates Act I, Scene 5.*

Repeating the solution here refreshes the idea for your audience, but now the solution means much more, because you spent the first three scenes of Act II describing why and how the solution is a good idea. This single statement actually summarizes all of the action you developed in Act II.

Next you'll create the climax of your presentation.

Act III, Scene 3: Setting Up the Climax

The *climax* of your presentation is where everything you've been saying comes together and you conclude your prepared remarks. You've been sailing toward this strong conclusion through the entire journey of your story up to this point. This climax sets the stage for the final resolution, which reflects the tone and spirit of your overall story, whether that's inspiration, danger, challenge, vision, courage, empowerment, or hope.

The content of this scene is what will appear on a slide while you provide the strong conclusion of your presentation. In the next cell, type a statement that describes the overarching theme of your concluding remarks, as shown in Figure 3-15.

Act III: Frame the resolution	
The crisis	Market conditions and regulations threaten a successful trip
The solution	Approve the IQ Pill marketing plan to sail there smoothly
The climax	Charting the course to financial results with the IQ Pill
The resolution	

Figure 3-15   *Act III, Scene 3 reiterates the nautical motif of the Contoso presentation.*

In the Contoso presentation "charting the course" reiterates the nautical motif, and the phrase "financial results with the IQ Pill," reestablishes what the audience wants to get from the presentation. You can bend Rule 1 from the section "Writing Using Three Ground Rules," in Chapter 2, by using a sentence fragment here. Whatever you write should be the minimum you need to simply convey the gist of your conclusion on a PowerPoint slide without distracting from the words you are saying.

Now that you have your climax, you're ready for the most anticipated scene in the entire presentation—the resolution of the situation.

Act III, Scene 4: Reaching the Resolution

Although you've made your closing remarks, the experience isn't over for your audience. They still need to take action by deciding whether they will accept your recommended solution. But before they decide, they'll probably want to discuss the situation, either in an informal dialogue with you or in a more formal question-and-answer session.

Act III, Scene 4 should frame the context for your conversation and the eventual resolution of your presentation by your audience. In the next cell, type a phrase that sets the tone for your conversation, as shown in Figure 3-16.

Act III: Frame the resolution	
The crisis	Market conditions and regulations threaten a successful trip
The solution	Approve the IQ Pill marketing plan to sail there smoothly
The climax	Charting the course to financial results with the IQ Pill
The resolution	The IQ Pill – Twice as smart in half the time

Figure 3-16 *Act III, Scene 5, featuring a simple slogan.*

This simple slogan, "The IQ Pill—Twice as smart in half the time," will be displayed on the screen during the question-and-answer session with your audience. Like your Scene 4 statement, this statement should be general and not controversial so that it subtly blends into the background and doesn't become the center of attention.

The completed Act III scenes form the end of your three-act story. They tie together the appeal to emotion in Act I, where you oriented your audience and got right to the heart of their problem, with the appeal to reason in Act II, where you targeted the rational component of the problem. Now that you've wrapped up all of the pieces in a coherent and elegant package, it's time for an initial script reading.

Reading Your PowerPoint Script Aloud

The most obvious benefit of your story template is that you can now see all of your ideas in one place and quickly grasp how each idea relates to the others. A printout of your story template at this point can also be used to guide you through an initial reading of your story to make sure that everything sounds right.

Review your story template before you print it. If it extends over multiple pages, you might need to split Act II into separate scenes that each fit on a page. To do this, position the pointer in any cell in the 5-Minute Column, and click **Table**, **Split Table** to split that row from the row above. If you change your mind, click **Edit**, **Undo Split Table**.

Stand with your printed story in hand so that you put yourself in a public speaking mode. You can read aloud privately in a conference room or ask your team to join you. After you read each statement from the printout, drop your hands to your sides, and then pause. Look ahead as if you're speaking to your audience and elaborate on the point you're making with the statement you just read. When you've finished, read the next point, and then drop your hands to your sides again and continue speaking.

REMEMBER Reading the statements of your story template aloud according to these directions helps you to avoid two of the most common problems in public speaking: talking to a piece of paper or a slide instead of the audience, and not being aware of what you're doing with your hands while you speak. When you read a statement from your printout and then drop your hands to your sides, you'll remember to speak to your audience every time you make a point. Although your hands might feel uncomfortable in this position, it's the best place for them to be while you speak. When you're ready to emphasize a specific point, raise an arm in a planned gesture to reinforce the point, and then drop your arm again.

If you completed all the cells in your story template, you have a total of 49 statements, which form the basis for a 45-minute presentation if you spend roughly one minute per slide. Begin by reading your Act I statements. Then read your Act II statements in the sequence in which you created them. Then read Act III. When you get to Scene 3, practice your concluding remarks. When you get to Scene 4, pause for a moment and think about questions that your audience might ask at this point.

Now that you've finished a full reading, read your script two more times in abbreviated versions. For the next reading, follow the same reading order as you did before, but this time, when you get to Act II, skip the *45-Minute Column* statements.

This leaves you with only 22 statements instead of 49, so if you spend about 40 seconds per statement, you'll finish in about 15 minutes. You'll still cover all the essential elements of your story; you're simply omitting one level of detail.

When you've finished, do a final reading. Follow the same reading order, but when you get to Act II, skip both the *15-Minute Column* and the *45-Minute Column* statements. This leaves you with 12 statements, so if you spend about 25 seconds per statement, you'll finish in about 5 minutes. In this case, you're omitting two levels of detail. Because you entered all of your statements in order of importance from top to bottom, if you

TIP   While you read your script aloud, keep a pen or pencil handy to jot down editing notes on your printout. You can update your story template later, when you return to your computer.

need to fine-tune the timing by deleting additional statements, you can do so by cutting from bottom to top in columns or sections of columns.

These three script readings demonstrate the formidable power you now have at your fingertips in your story template. You maintain the integrity of your story structure whether you have 45, 15, or 5 minutes for your script reading, and you can carry forward this benefit to your PowerPoint slides when you set up your storyboard in Chapter 4.

Reviewing Your Script with Your Team

Just as you can use your story template to see and manage all of your statements at a glance, other people can use it to review your story too. If you're working with only a few people, you can simply display the story template on your computer screen and make edits together. If you're working with a larger group and want to call a meeting to review your sentences, send a copy of the story template Word document through e-mail to all of the members of the team in advance.

IMPORTANT   Don't move forward from this stage of the process until you finalize your story template and get agreement from everyone who has a stake in your presentation.

At this point, it's absolutely essential that you get agreement on the story template from anyone who has a stake in the presentation. This includes the members of your team, people in other departments of your organization, and anyone who needs to give clearance and approval for what you'll say.

Using your story template as a review document, you can easily make quick adjustments to your wording or structure and invite others to contribute their expertise and take ownership in the success of your presentation. Getting approval on your story template allows everyone to focus on your ideas instead of on design issues, which could prove distracting at this point. When you get final approval of the structure and sequence of your story up front, you'll reduce the likelihood that you'll need to spend unnecessary time and effort later, after you've invested time in the design process.

When you meet with Contoso CEO Chris Gray on Wednesday to review how you'll move the marketing presentation beyond bullet points, print copies of your story template and bring them to the meeting. Talk through the ideas in the order in which you rehearsed them, and discuss the options you have to scale down the story if your presentation time is reduced from 45 minutes to 15 or 5. When Chris is happy with the direction of your story template, you're ready to take the next step beyond bullet points.

Lowering the Curtain on Your Story Template

You accomplish a number of sophisticated things with your completed story template. You find focus with a classical three-act story structure. You appeal to emotion and reason. You create dramatic conflict, which will keep your audience interested. You select and organize your ideas in a structure and a sequence that helps people to pay attention to and remember the information you're providing.

Before you move on to the next major step in the Beyond Bullet Points approach—storyboarding your script—read through the following 10 tips to find ideas that might improve your story template.

10 Tips for Enhancing Your Story Template

With your story template in hand, you can rest assured that you have a focused tale to tell at your next presentation. When you're comfortable with the basics of completing your template, try improvising on the concept using these 10 tips.

Tip 1: The Power of Three

As much as you might want to load up your PowerPoint slides with data, the quantity of information that people can understand is always constrained by the mind's limited ability to handle it. You can help your audience to understand information better by presenting your ideas in groups of three. Research has found that on average people can hold three or four independent ideas in short-term memory at a time. (See the article *"The Science of Making Your PowerPoint Memorable: Q&A with Nelson Cowan,"* available at *www.sociablemedia.com*.)

Your story template helps you to organize your ideas in groups of three in multiple ways. Your entire story consists of three acts. Act II contains three main ideas, listed in the 5-Minute Column. Each main idea has three supporting points, listed in the 15-Minute Column. Each 15-Minute Column point has three supporting points as well, listed in the 45-Minute Column. It might be challenging to boil down your statements to groups of three in this structure, but your hard work will pay off: your audience will more easily absorb, remember, and understand your ideas.

Tip 2: Making Room for Four

Although three is a powerful number, you might find while working in Act II of your story template that you have four points to make in a column. Instead of manually inserting cells into the Word table, you can go to *www.sociablemedia.com* and download a free version of the story template that includes four rows in all of the Act II sections instead of three. As with the three-row version of the story template described in this chapter, if you have fewer points to make in any section than you have cells, you can simply leave the cells blank. The disadvantage of using a template with four levels of support is that the number of cells increases from 49 to 94, significantly increasing the size and complexity of your presentation. Keep in mind that the more points you have, the more time you need and the more information people need to process. To avoid long and complicated presentations, try to stick to three points rather than four.

Tip 3: Variations on a Theme

The story template described in this chapter is a basic structure that you can tailor to your needs as you become more comfortable with the process. For example, sometimes in any of your column headings, you might answer the question *what* if it's a better fit than the most commonly used questions *why* and *how*. When you've mastered the fundamentals of Act II of your story template in this chapter, feel free to improvise on the theme in a way that works best for your presentations.

Tip 4: Grow Clarity Using a Logic Tree

Act II of your story template is based on a classical technique called a *logic tree*, which dates back at least 1,700 years. A logic tree, also called a *tree diagram*, shows the relationships between levels of ideas in a hierarchy—the basic look of the logic tree diagram is recognizable today in the form of an organizational chart. Applying a logic tree to your ideas is a powerful way to distill them to their essence and arrange them in a hierarchy. Act II of your story template is inspired by a logic tree— you can see the logic tree form if you turn the story template on its side and put your solution at the top of the tree, as shown in Figure 3-17.

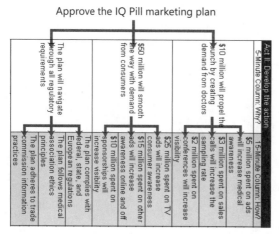

Figure 3-17   *Act II of the story template turned on its side to show its structure as a logic tree.*

You can explore the concepts of logic diagramming in more detail in a number of sources. For example, Marya W. Holcombe and Judith K. Stein provide a good introduction to building a logical structure for presentations in Chapter 4 of *Presentations for Decision Makers, Third Edition* (Wiley, 1996), and Barbara Minto devotes an entire book to a sophisticated, thorough, and comprehensive application of this technique in *The Minto Pyramid Principle: Logic in Writing, Thinking, and Problem Solving* (Minto International, 1996).

These resources explain how to group similar ideas and work from the details at the bottom of a hierarchy up to the main ideas at the top. By incorporating these concepts as you develop your skills with your story template, you'll find clarity before you know it.

Tip 5: Build an Outline in a Brainstorm

Your Act II statements have to come from somewhere. If they don't flow easily from your imagination, you might need to loosen things up with a little brainstorming. A number of excellent books and online resources such as *www.innovationtools.com*, are available to help you to brainstorm new ideas either on your own or with your team. Whatever technique you decide to use, you need to understand the relationship between the fruit of your brainstorming labor and the story template process you undertake in Act II.

Brainstorming is the art of generating ideas for a particular purpose; it supports an environment of free-flowing thinking without constraints. *Presentation development* is the art of selecting and prioritizing ideas; it calls on a different set of skills, including critical thinking, selection, prioritization, and reasoning.

When you've finished your brainstorming exercises, the story template helps you to select the ideas that best support the focus of your presentation. As you begin to work on Act II, gather all of the brainstorming ideas you might have on hand, whether they're in the form of lists, note cards, whiteboard diagrams, or other formats. Then apply the process of writing your Act II statements described in this chapter.

At times, you might need to switch back into a brainstorming mode when you're stuck on a statement or if your Act II structure isn't working. But when you've generated fresh ideas, it's time to switch back into story template mode so that you can select appropriate ideas that support the focus of your presentation.

Brainstorming and using the story template are different but complementary techniques, and when you alternate the two, you can have the best of both worlds—the correct selection of the freshest ideas that support your singular story.

Tip 6: Tap Your Team's Talents

Consider working with your team to structure your ideas in Act II. By connecting a projector to your computer, you can display a number of software tools that allow you to work with your team to develop your Act II statements. As mentioned, you can project your story template on a screen as a Word document and modify your statements in real time. Or you can build your own tables or logic trees (see "Tip 4: Grow Clarity Using a Logic Tree") using Microsoft Visio, Microsoft OneNote, or PowerPoint's organizational chart feature.

If you don't have a projector or you prefer a hands-on approach, use a sheet of paper, a flip chart, or a whiteboard to draw your logic tree. Or write your draft Act II statements on sticky notes and affix them to a wall to build a logic tree, as described in David Straker's *Rapid Problem Solving with Post-it Notes* (Fisher Books, 1997). Experiment with a range of techniques and tools until you find what works best for you and your team to focus and prioritize your ideas. When you've finished, return to your Word document and enter your statements in the story template.

When it comes to creating the story template, you'll probably find that tapping into the talents of your team will build the best presentation possible.

Tip 7: Taking the Express Elevator

When entrepreneurs begin to approach investors to raise money for a venture, they're expected to have something called an *elevator pitch*. The idea is that they pitch their company within the length of time of an elevator ride. Even if you're not trying to raise money for your company, you might need to give your own version of an elevator pitch if you get a call from your boss before you give your presentation and she says, "I'm sorry but I can't make it to your presentation—can you tell me quickly what you're going to say?"

In every case, you'll be clear about what you're going to say after you complete your story template. To respond to your boss, give your own elevator pitch by first summarizing your Act I scenes. Then describe each of your main 5-Minute Column points in Act II of your story template. This sets the context for the presentation and covers the high-level points. If your boss is interested in knowing more about any particular point, you can elaborate more as needed by providing more supporting information from the 15- and 45-minute columns.

This handy technique is not just for elevator pitches and verbal summaries. If you have to write the marketing description for your talk, you've got the outline already written in the story template in the form of your Act I and Act II, 5-Minute Column statements. If you want to let other people know the structure of your talk in advance, you can summarize it in the same way in an e-mail message. In all of these situations, your story template can keep you speeding along with effective communication.

Tip 8: The Outline of Convention

If you're more comfortable writing out your Act II scenes in linear form rather than using the story template, try an *action outline* instead. With an action outline, you follow all of the same steps and principles as you do with the story template, but you use standard outlining conventions of indentation instead of the cells of a table. Here's how Act II of the Contoso story template would look in an action outline:

Approve the IQ marketing plan and we'll sail there smoothly. (*Why?*)

1 $10 million will propel the launch by creating demand from doctors. (*How?*)

   a $5 million spent on ads will increase medical awareness. (*Why?*)

   i Similar spending levels helped us to reach our targets in the past.

   ii Industry averages validate the projected results.

   iii Ad agency figures predict that ad responses will remain stable.

   b $3 million spent on sales calls will increase the sampling rate. (*Why?*)

   i Our current program resulted in a 20% increase in sampling.

   ii The sales call program for Company X has been performing well.

   iii Based on comparable pills, we can expect to meet our goals.

   c $2 million spent on conferences will increase visibility. (*Why?*)

   i At other conferences, we measured a 24 percent increase in visibility.

   ii The schedule ensures that top decision makers will attend.

   iii Our sales reps report good results from previous sponsorships.

2 $50 million will smooth the way with demand from consumers. (*How?*)

   ■ *Supporting points here.*

3 The plan will navigate through all regulatory requirements. (*How?*)

   ■ *Supporting points here.*

The title of this outline repeats the solution from Act I, Scene 5, in the story template, and the first numbered level corresponds to the 5-Minute Column in Act II. The next levels of indentation correspond to the 15-Minute Column and the 45-Minute Column. This type of outlining accomplishes the same thing as Act II of the story template but in a linear way. Choose the technique that works for you, whether or not it's conventional.

Tip 9: Cascading Conclusions

To present more clearly, start thinking upside-down. Where you might have analyzed details before coming to a conclusion, your story template flips that process around, giving the conclusion first and the supporting details after. If you present all of the details first, your audience might have to struggle to retain that information until they know where your presentation is going. But when you state your conclusion first, the audience remembers that single idea, setting the context for all the details to follow.

You set up the conclusion as a recommended solution in Act I and follow it with supporting details in the first three scenes of Act II. The same technique works within the Act II scenes when you present a main point in the 5-Minute Column before presenting the supporting details in the 15-Minute Column, and then present a point in the 15-Minute Column before presenting its supporting details in the 45-Minute Column.

When you invert your usual way of thinking and present your conclusion first and supporting details later, people will more easily remember and understand what you say. You couldn't ask for a better conclusion.

Tip 10: The Invisible Story Structure

As it turns out, when you make your structure invisible, your story becomes clearer. You never hear the characters in film say, "This is the beginning, this is the middle, and this is the end." Most film scripts are written using a three-act structure similar to the story template. Whether or not they're aware of it, audiences find a film satisfying if the classical elements of a story are embedded in a screenplay and invisible on screen. Because your story is built using this classical structure, you don't need to tell your audience when you are at the beginning, middle, or end of your presentation. Your story structure is completely interwoven with your story template in a way that your sophisticated and media-savvy audience can understand without prompting.

Chapter 4: **Preparing and Planning Your Storyboard**

In this chapter, you will:

1. Transform your script into a storyboard.

2. Add storyboard guides.

3. Plan for the visuals you'll project on-screen.

4. Write out the words you'll speak.

5. Review your acts and scenes.

The empty screen that you face when you start Microsoft Office PowerPoint can be daunting if you don't know where to begin. You won't have this experience because when you complete the Beyond Bullet Points Story Template, you have in hand a complete and coherent story that sets the foundation for all of your slides. Next you'll transfer the statements from the story template to PowerPoint, where you'll transform them into a storyboard that you'll use to plan your spoken words and projected visuals.

Introducing the Storyboard

If you were a Hollywood director who was planning a film, you'd probably hire a storyboard artist to sketch frames of selected scenes from your script. These initial sketches enable everyone on the production team to begin to see how the film will look so that they can start to turn the words from the script into spoken words and projected images. A storyboard is a powerful tool because it lets you see many frames from a story in a single view and consider how those frames relate to one another through a narrative. Without this important perspective, you wouldn't be able to see how the parts link together to become a coherent whole.

You won't need to hire a storyboard artist or sketch anything to create your PowerPoint storyboard. Instead you'll adapt the basic techniques of creating a Hollywood storyboard to help you to manage the big picture of your own story. This will shift your thinking of a PowerPoint presentation from individual slides toward slides related as frames in a strip of film. By setting up a new PowerPoint file in this way, you'll use the storyboard not only to plan your words and visuals but also to present them to the audience using a single media document that works across projector, paper, and browser.

The first step in this process is to prepare the storyboard by sending the statements in the story template to PowerPoint.

Transferring Your Script to PowerPoint

As you complete the three acts of the story template, you're actually also formatting the information in a specific way that prepares it for a PowerPoint storyboard. The same concise statements that communicate each act and scene in the story template are the concise statements that will communicate clearly to the audience in the title area of the PowerPoint slides, as shown in Figure 4-1.

Writing statements for both the story template and the PowerPoint slides is the powerful fulcrum that allows you to leverage the conventional PowerPoint approach beyond bullet points into a new world of visual storytelling. This process embeds your script in a storyboard and ensures that everything you say and show maps back to the structure and sequence of a story.

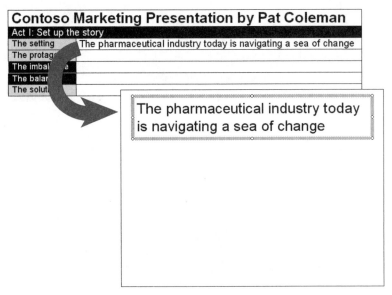

Figure 4-1 *Transferring a statement from the story template to the title area of a PowerPoint slide.*

In the original Contoso presentation, as in most PowerPoint presentations, the title area always contained category headings.

There's no escaping bullet points when you use category headings, because each heading exists to head the categorical list of bullet points below it. If you placed only a category heading on a slide without bullet points, it wouldn't tell you much, and you'd have trouble illustrating it. But when you place a statement from the story template in the title area, the statement establishes the meaning of the slide and prepares the way for a visual in the slide area below.

The best way to describe the statements you place on the slides is by using a term from journalism: *headlines*. Like newspaper headlines, the statements communicate to an audience using simple, clear, and direct language in a conversational tone within the constraints of limited space.

When you send all of the statements in the story template to a new PowerPoint file, you ensure that you never have to face an empty screen when you begin creating a presentation. Instead you'll always start with a set of PowerPoint slides, each of which already contains a meaningful headline.

Sending the Story Template from Word to PowerPoint

You send the story template statements to a new PowerPoint file using a little-known feature in Microsoft Word, the **Send to Microsoft Office PowerPoint** command.

But before you use this feature, you need to do some preparation work on the Word document. First save the story template, then click **Edit**, **Select All** to select all of the statements in the template, and then click **Edit**, **Copy**.

Next create a new Word document, position the cursor in the document, and click **Edit**, **Paste Special**. In the **Paste Special** dialog box, select **Unformatted Text** and click OK. The resulting new document should look similar to Figure 4-2.

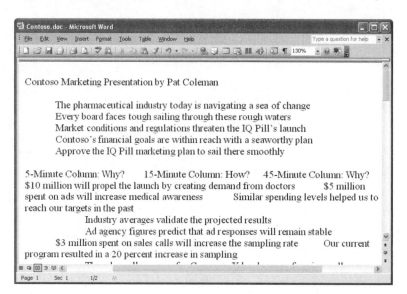

Figure 4-2 *Initial view after pasting statements from the story template into a new Word document.*

Delete the line containing the title and byline and also the line containing the column headings. Next remove any extra spaces between words and add new line breaks where needed so that you end up with only one statement per line, as shown in Figure 4-3.

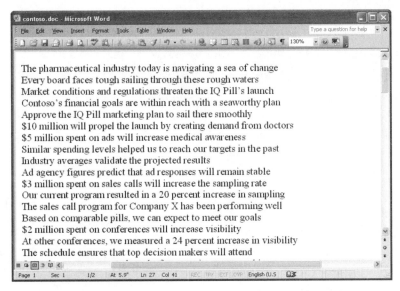

Figure 4-3 *View of Word document with extra spaces between words removed, new line breaks added, and only one statement per line.*

Next click **File**, **Send To**, and click **Microsoft Office PowerPoint**. This opens a new PowerPoint file and inserts each statement in the title area of its own slide, as shown in Figure 4-4. Click **File**, **Save**, name the new PowerPoint file, and save it on your local computer. As in this example, some of the statements might not fit perfectly in the title area. You'll address that problem next by setting up the Slide Master.

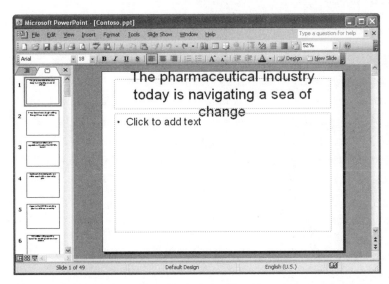

Figure 4-4 *Initial view of new PowerPoint file with a statement from the story template in the title area of a slide.*

Setting Up the Slide Master

Now that you've transferred the statements from the story template to a new PowerPoint file, the next step is to set up the Slide Master. You use the Slide Master to specify the formatting for the slides in a presentation, so any changes you make here will be automatically applied to both existing and new slides created from the master. After you transfer the story template to a new PowerPoint file, follow these steps to format the Slide Master.

To format the Slide Master for the storyboard

1   Click **View**, **Master**, **Slide Master**. Click the **Click here to edit Master title style** placeholder in the title area at the top of the slide, and on the **Formatting** toolbar, click the **Font** drop-down arrow and select **Arial**, and then click the **Font Size** drop-down arrow and select **40**.

> **TIP**   Instead of formatting the presentation every time you send the story template from Word to PowerPoint, go to www.sociablemedia.com to download a free Beyond Bullet Points Storyboard Formatter. To use it, follow the instructions in Appendix B.

2   With the title area still selected, click **Format, Placeholder**, and then click the **Text Box** tab in the **Format AutoShape** dialog box. Make sure that the **Word Wrap Text in AutoShape** check box is selected select **Top** in the **Text Anchor Point** drop-down list, and click OK.

3   With the title area still selected, on the **Formatting** toolbar, click **Align Left**.

4   Delete the **Date Area**, **Footer Area**, and **Number Area** placeholders at the bottom of the Slide Master.

5   Click the **Object Area** placeholder to select it, and then click and drag the sizing handle at the bottom of the object area to expand the object area to the bottom of the slide, leaving a margin equal to the margin at the top of the slide. Delete all of the text inside the object area, and with the object area still selected, click the **Bullets** button on the **Formatting** toolbar to remove the bullet formatting. Your screen should look similar to Figure 4-5.

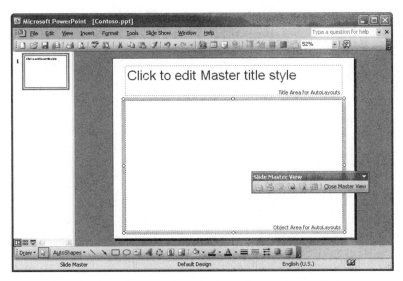

Figure 4-5 *The final Slide Master with all new formatting applied.*

6 Click the **Close Master View** button on the **Slide Master View** toolbar to return to the previous view of the slides.

These formatting changes applied to the Slide Master establish the foundation for a clean and basic slide area for all of the slides, which aligns with the research-based design principles described in Appendix A. If you return to reformat the Slide Master later, always leave the background white. And if you modify the title area, make sure that the font style and size you choose allow you to clearly read the headlines in Slide Sorter view—otherwise, you undermine your ability to manage the slides as a storyboard. Before you modify the Slide Master, consider the issues related to formatting masters described in "Tip 7: Customize the Beyond Bullet Points Storyboard Formatter," later in this chapter.

SEE ALSO If you want to adjust or align the placeholders on the Slide Master more precisely, click View, Grid and Guides and specify the settings that meet your needs. For more information, see "Tip 1: Layouts Beyond the Basics," in Chapter 4.

Click **View**, **Slide Sorter** to see a first draft of your new PowerPoint storyboard. In this view, you can see thumbnail-size versions of all of the slides in a single window, as shown in Figure 4-6. At this early stage, the PowerPoint file already passes the first analysis test from Chapter 1: you can quickly see the focus of the presentation by reading only the slide titles.

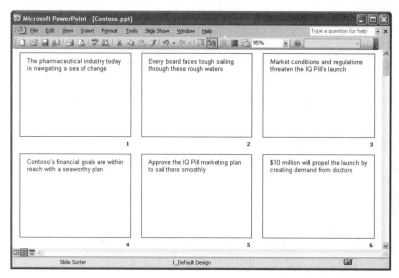

Figure 4-6   *Slide Sorter view, with headlines clearly visible.*

Changing the Slide Layout

Using the Beyond Bullet Points approach, you no longer have any need for bullet points, so you can reformat the layout of all the slides to encourage a visual approach. You'll add graphics to each of the slides in Chapters 5 and 6.

To change the layout of all the slides in Slide Sorter view, click **Edit**, **Select All**, click **Format**, **Slide Layout**, and click the **Title and Content** layout to apply that layout to all of the selected slides, as shown in Figure 4-7.

Congratulations! You have now officially moved beyond bullet points. Even before you've added a single visual, the PowerPoint file is embedded with a strong story, meaningful headlines anchoring every slide, and a basic layout designed to hold graphical elements in the main area of the slides instead of bullet points.

As you review the slide titles in Slide Sorter view, you might find that some of the statements extend beyond the two-line limit. To fix that and any other problems, you'll need to master the basics of editing headlines next.

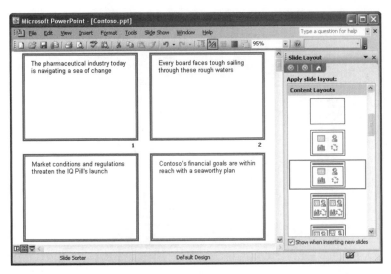

Figure 4-7   *Reformatting the layout of all of the slides to encourage a visual approach.*

Editing the Headlines

PowerPoint provides two ways for you to edit headlines. The first method is to click **View**, **Normal**, click in the title area of the slide, and start editing. The second method is to view the presentation in Outline format, shown in Figure 4-8. In Normal view, the leftmost pane of the PowerPoint window contains two tabs: **Outline** and **Slides**. When you click the **Outline** tab, you'll see a list of headlines, and to the left of each headline, a number and a small icon of a slide. Click in the text of the headline you want to edit. As you make changes to a headline on the **Outline** tab, the corresponding text in the title area of the slide to the right is updated. In this example, the phrase "a sea" has been selected and edited to read "an ocean."

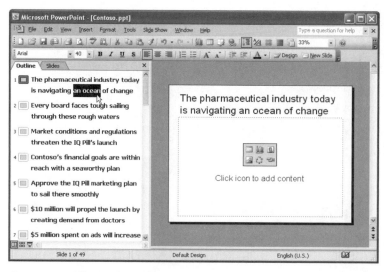

Figure 4-8   *Editing a headline on the Outline tab.*

You can drag the vertical line at the right side of the **Outline** pane to increase or decrease its size to accommodate the width of the headlines. The **Outline** tab can be useful for reviewing all of the headlines of the slides in a list that you can read from top to bottom. Later you can print this outline to use as speaker notes.

Scroll through all of the slides, and when you find a headline that exceeds the two-line limit of the title area, edit the headline using the techniques described here. Sometimes you can reduce a headline's length simply by deleting a word or two, without affecting its meaning. At other times, you might have to revise and restructure a headline to make it fit. Always stick with the two-line limit for headlines to maintain consistency in the presentation, to leave ample room for visuals, and to challenge yourself to be as concise as possible.

Now that you've transformed the story template into a storyboard, it's time to start preparing it by adding some slides.

Preparing Your Storyboard

Click **View**, **Slide Sorter** to take a look at the starting point for your storyboard. Before you start working with the presentation in this form, add some additional slides to round out your story and make managing the slides easier.

Adding a Title and Closing Credits

Every Hollywood film begins with an opening title, and your PowerPoint presentation should have one too. In Slide Sorter view, locate the slide with the Act III, Scene 3 statement, in the second to last position in the storyboard. This slide summarizes the emotional engine that drives your story forward—in the Contoso example, the headline is *Charting the course to financial results with the IQ Pill*. This headline can also make an interesting and intriguing title for your story, especially if the audience doesn't know much about the presentation in advance. To create a title slide from this slide, select the slide, press **Ctrl+D**, and then click and drag the duplicate slide to the first slide position in the presentation.

Double-click the new slide to work with it in Normal view. After the last word in the headline, type a colon and then the title of the story template. In the Contoso example, the headline is now *Charting the course to financial results with the IQ Pill: Contoso Marketing Presentation by Pat Coleman*, as shown in Figure 4-9. You now have the basis for the presentation title slide, which you'll finish designing in Chapter 6.

Next return to Slide Sorter view, position the cursor to the right of the last slide in the presentation, and click **Insert, New Slide** to add a blank slide to contain the closing credits. Double-click the new slide to work with it in Normal view. In the title area, type a note to yourself describing the image you'd like to add to this slide later—this will be the image that the audience keeps in their minds after the presentation is over. The image might include your organization's name, your contact information, a Web site address, or a simple visual that conveys the theme of the presentation. Like the title slide, you'll complete the design of this slide in Chapter 6.

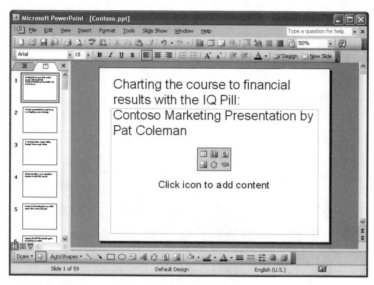

Figure 4-9   *The new title slide.*

Next it's time to find some guidance in the storyboard.

Creating Storyboard Guides

With a large number of slides in the storyboard, it can be difficult to distinguish between the acts and scenes when you look at presentations in Slide Sorter view. You can make your job easier by adding storyboard guides, which are "hidden" placeholder slides that are used to indicate the major sections and subsections of the storyboard. You'll be able to see these slides when you work in the storyboard, but they won't appear when you run the presentation. Storyboard Guides help keep the entire presentation organized in your own mind so that you can explain things clearly to the audience.

TIP   Instead of creating storyboard guides from scratch, go to *www.sociablemedia.com* to download a free set of predesigned Beyond Bullet Points Storyboard Guides.

Before you start working with the storyboard, create a set of hidden storyboard guides that will help you to manage the slides more easily by following these steps.

To create hidden storyboard guides

1 In Slide Sorter view, position the cursor to the right of the last slide in the presentation, which is the closing credits slide you just created. Click **Insert, New Slide** to add a blank slide.

2 Double-click the new slide to work with it in Normal view. Click **Format, Slide Layout**, and select the Blank layout format.

3 On the Drawing toolbar, click the Text Box button, and then drag the cursor from left to right across the entire screen to create the text box. Type **Act II, Scene 3** in the box, and then select the box by clicking its frame. On the **Formatting** toolbar, click **Center**, and then click the **Size** drop-down arrow and click **88**. Then click the **Font Color** drop-down arrow, and select white.

4 Click **Format, Background**, and choose black in the **Color** drop-down list and click **Apply**. Your screen should look like Figure 4-10. Changing the background color of the slide to a dark color like black makes it easy to see these guides among the other white slides in the storyboard, and changing the font color to white, as you did in step 3, makes it possible to read the white text against the black background.

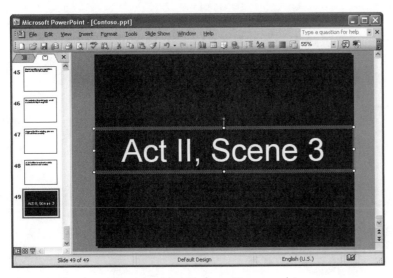

Figure 4-10 *A storyboard guide with formatting complete.*

5   Click **View**, **Slide Sorter**, and select the slide you just created. Press Ctrl+D four times to create four duplicates of the slide. Double-click the first slide, and in Normal view, edit the text on this slide and the next slides in sequence so that the five slides contain the following text:

- Act I

- Act II, Scene 1

- Act II, Scene 2

- Act II, Scene 3

- Act III

6   Click **View**, **Slide Sorter,** select the first storyboard guide, hold down Shift, and click the last storyboard guide. With the five slides selected, right-click any slide, and click **Hide Slide**, as shown in Figure 4-11. The storyboard guides are now hidden, which means that they're not visible when you click **View**, **Slide Show** to run the presentation. Because the storyboard guides don't appear on screen during the presentation, you can always leave them in the PowerPoint file as they are. If you don't want the storyboard guides to appear when you print the storyboard, clear the **Print Hidden Slides** check box in the **Print** dialog box.

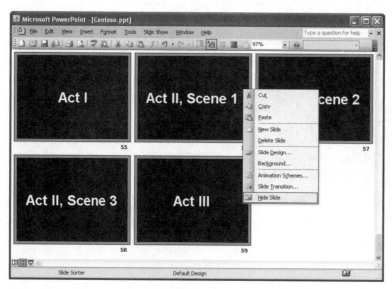

Figure 4-11   *Applying the **Hide Slide** feature to all of the storyboard guides.*

When you use the **Hide Slide** feature, a hidden slide icon appears, with the slide number inside, as shown in Figure 4-12. Be careful to never put a hidden slide in the first position in the presentation—in that instance, the slide will be visible on screen.

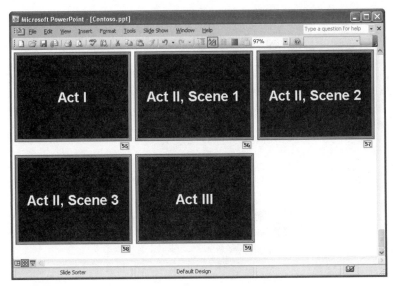

Figure 4-12   *With the Hide Slide feature applied, the slide number changes to a hidden slide icon.*

Now that you have your hidden storyboard guides, it's time to put them in their places.

Repositioning the Storyboard Guides

The storyboard guides let you quickly see the relevant acts and scenes in Slide Sorter view. As you reposition the guides, you'll also check to make sure that the slides are in the same order as when you rehearsed the lines of the PowerPoint script in the section "Reading Your PowerPoint Script Aloud," in Chapter 3.

After you create the storyboard guides, follow these steps to reposition them in their appropriate locations according to the sequence of slides established in the story template.

To reposition the storyboard guides

1 Using the story template as a reference, drag the Act I storyboard guide to the left of the first scene of Act I.

2 Review the headlines in the first five slides to make sure that they are in the same order as the story template. Then drag the Act II, Scene 1 guide to the left of the first Act II, 5-Minute Column slide, as shown in Figure 4-13.

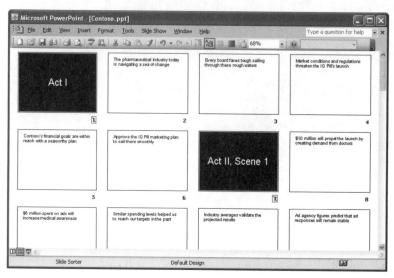

Figure 4-13 *Two storyboard guides after repositioning.*

3 Review the next series of slides to verify that they follow the order of the story template. If you need to change the order of a slide, drag it to its new position. When you reach the second 5-Minute Column headline, drag the Act II, Scene 2 guide to the left of it.

4 Review the next series of slides until you reach the third 5-Minute Column headline, and then drag the Act II, Scene 3 guide to the left of it.

5 Review the next series of slides until you reach Act II, Scene 4. Then drag the Act III guide to the left of the first Act III slide.

To indicate the sections of the storyboard in even greater detail, you can create additional storyboard guides that mark the positions of slides that correspond to the 15-Minute Column and 45-Minute Column of the story template. This level of detail comes in handy if your presentation time is reduced and you need to quickly scale down the number of slides you'll show while still keeping the integrity of your story. See "Tip 2: Scale to Time," later in this chapter, to find out how.

Now that you have the main storyboard guides in place, whenever you are in Slide Sorter view, you can see at a glance the main sections of the presentation. But the storyboard not only helps you to see and manage the slides in Slide Sorter view, it can also help you to see and manage your spoken words using a lesser-known PowerPoint view.

Planning Your Spoken Words

No PowerPoint slide is an island, because it always exists in the context of your spoken words. To create a coherent presentation, you need to plan not only the slides but also the words you speak while you project the slide on a screen. You do this using a little-known PowerPoint view called Notes Page. Before taking a tour of the Notes Page view features, you should first set up the Notes Master.

Setting Up the Notes Master

Just as the Slide Master sets the formatting for all of the slides, the Notes Master sets the formatting for all of the notes pages. By making a few adjustments to the Notes Master, you'll be able to use the notes pages to effectively plan both your slides and your spoken words.

Before you plan the way the slides relate to your spoken words, you should follow these steps to format the Notes Master.

TIP   To save time formatting the Notes Master, go to *www.sociablemedia.com* to download the free Beyond Bullet Points Storyboard Formatter. To use it, follow the instructions in Appendix B.

To format the Notes Master

1 Click **View**, **Master**, **Notes Master**, and select the slide placeholder in the top half of the page. Click **Format**, **Placeholder**, and in the **Format Placeholder** dialog box, click the **Size** tab. Select the **Lock Aspect Ratio** check box, change the **Width** setting in the **Size And Rotate** area to **6"**, and click **OK**. The **Height** setting will be automatically adjusted to *4.5", as shown in Figure 4-14*.

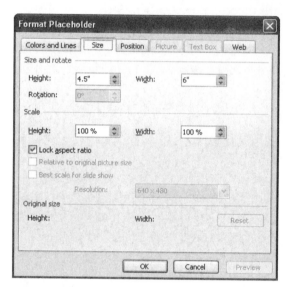

Figure 4-14   *Select Lock Aspect Ratio to preserve the shape of the slide placeholder.*

2 Select the **Notes Body Area** box in the bottom half of the tab, and click **Format**, **Placeholder**. In the **Format AutoShape** dialog box, clear the **Lock Aspect Ratio** check box, make sure that **Height** is set to **4.5"** and **Width** is set to **6"**, and click **OK**. You can change font styles and sizes here later if you want.

NOTE   Placing your logo on the Notes Master ensures that you extend your organization's brand across the printed materials. Doing this keeps the logo out of the slide area, where it can easily distract the audience from your ideas or dramatically reduce the creative options available to you on the screen. To review research supporting this recommendation, see Appendix A.

3 Insert your logo in the Notes Master if you want to include it somewhere in the PowerPoint file. You can also edit or delete any other Notes Master placeholders, including the **Header Area**, **Date Area**, **Footer Area**, and **Number Area**. In this example, the Contoso logo has been added in the lower-left corner, the **Number Area** remains in the lower-right corner, and the **Header Area** and **Date Area** have been deleted from the top of the page.

4 Hold down **Shift** while you click both the slide placeholder and the **Notes Body Area**, and on the **Drawing** toolbar, click **Draw**, **Align or Distribute**, **Align Center**. Then click and drag to position the two boxes on the page so that they align vertically and horizontally with the spacing you want. If you want to align any placeholders on the Notes Master more precisely, click **View, Grid and Guides**, and configure the settings according to your needs

5 Select only the slide placeholder again, click **Format**, **Placeholder**, click the **Colors and Lines** tab, select **Line,** and in the **Color** drop-down list, and select **No Line**, as shown in Figure 4-15, and then click **OK**.

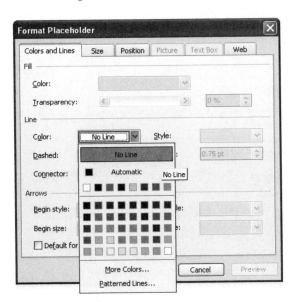

Figure 4-15 *Select No Line to remove the line surrounding the slide placeholder.*

Your screen should now look similar to Figure 4-16; the slide placeholder is selected in this figure so that you can see its outer boundaries.

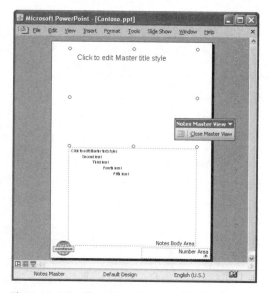

Figure 4-16   *The Notes Master, with all reformatting completed.*

6   Click **Close Master View** to return to the previous view.

Now let's take a look at a specific notes page in the Contoso presentation.

Writing Your Narrative

Select any slide in the storyboard, and then click **View**, **Notes Page** to display a typical notes page, as shown in Figure 4-17. The box in the top half of the page shows the slide as it will appear on screen during the presentation. At this point, you can see only the headline in the title area of the slide. In Chapters 5 and 6 you'll add a graphic below the headline when you design the slide in Normal view.

The box in the bottom half of the page is a text box linked to the slide above that does not appear on screen during the presentation. You can type text here as you normally would in any text box.

To tap into the power of Notes Page view, review the slide headline in the top half of the page, and then write out what you plan to say about this headline in the text box, as shown in the magnified view of the notes area in Figure 4-18.

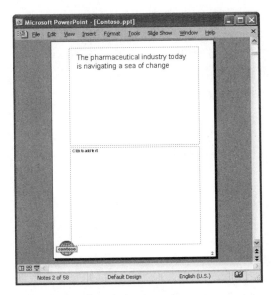

Figure 4-17 *A typical notes page.*

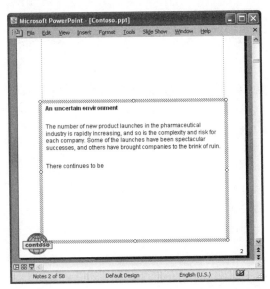

Figure 4-18 *A magnified view of the notes area in Notes Page view, displaying an idea being described in complete sentences and paragraphs.*

It's important to write out what you'll say about the headline in complete sentences and paragraphs. Fully writing out your ideas in the notes area fleshes out the ideas and increases your confidence in the topic. It also helps you to develop an intimate connection with the headline, which will aid you later when you speak. During the presentation, the headline will show the audience in a glance the idea of the slide, and it will also prompt you to improvise on the detailed written explanation, with a relaxed voice that comes from knowing the topic so well. And when you've written out the explanation of each slide, you can create an effective handout, as you'll see in Chapters 5 and 6.

In the notes area, spell out as much of your explanation as you can at this stage of the presentation. If you're pressed for time, you can jot down brief notes at this point and then expand on them in more detail later as you design the storyboard or develop it for production.

REMEMBER Start writing out your spoken words in the notes area in Notes Page view so that you establish the complete context for what you'll say. You can continue to add notes in this view, in the notes area in Normal view, or even in Slide Sorter view, as described in "Tip 9: Write in Slide Sorter View," later in this chapter.

Now that you've prepared and reviewed the PowerPoint file, it's time to start storyboarding, keeping a few ground rules in mind.

Storyboarding Using Three Ground Rules

Your new PowerPoint storyboard is inspired by the idea of a Hollywood storyboard, but it's actually a much more sophisticated tool than its namesake. What you've created is the foundation for a complete, integrated, and coherent media document that manages both the words you speak and the visuals you show on screen. For a quick tour of its capabilities, take a look at the PowerPoint presentation in the three storyboarding views: Slide Sorter, Notes Page, and Normal.

In Slide Sorter view, you can see the complete story as a sequence of thumbnail-size images that flow evenly from one slide to the next. In Notes Page view, you can not only see a specific slide at any point in the flow of the presentation, but you can also write out the words you'll speak when you display that slide. And in Normal view, you can add a visual element to each of the slides in the storyboard. Together these three views form the PowerPoint storyboard that you'll use to design and produce the live presentation.

As you review and work with the powerful new storyboard tool, three ground rules can help you and your audience to stay connected to the big picture.

Rule 1: Keep Reviewing the Big Picture

When you work with the storyboard, keep in mind that *it's all about the story*. You've ensured that's the case by following the procedures in the Beyond Bullet Points approach. After you send the statements in the story template to PowerPoint, each PowerPoint slide becomes a specific piece of that story that you can now see in the storyboard. When you add the storyboard guides, the major story sections become clear, and you can see the beginning, middle, and end of the story.

As you work with a presentation, be sure to regularly review the big picture of your story in Slide Sorter view. By doing this you avoid concentrating exclusively on only single slides; instead you focus on what is happening *across* slides. By staying connected to the single main narrative of the presentation, your confidence and authority will come across in everything you say and show. To maintain this connection, you should return to Slide Sorter view often to review what's happening in each act and scene and to continually review how an individual slide relates to the whole story.

While you're working on the storyboard, look for ways to keep the story on track. For example, if you're concerned that in Act II the audience might forget the purpose for the presentation you established in Act I, you can add slides throughout the storyboard to refresh their memory. For details, see "Tip 1: Remind the Audience of Your Purpose," later in this chapter.

TIP   To change the size of the slides in Slide Sorter view, on the Standard toolbar, click the Zoom drop-down arrow, and click the magnification you want.

Whatever techniques you try, remember to return to the big picture view to see how you can improve the audience's understanding of the story.

Rule 2: Maintain a Steady Pace

When you send the story template from Word to PowerPoint, you break up the story evenly into slides that flow smoothly from one to the next in the order you established in the template. Remember, you should think about the slides in the storyboard as individual frames in a strip of movie film. This "filmstrip" represents the story in the story template. Because every frame in the filmstrip contains a similar amount of information, you'll maintain a steady pace in the presentation as you deliver the slides in equal time increments.

If you complete three columns in Act II of the story template, you end up with a storyboard with 49 slides for a 45-minute presentation, which sets a pace of about one minute per slide. If you complete two columns, you end up with 22 slides, which sets a pace of about 40 seconds for each slide in a 15-minute presentation. And if you complete only one column, you have 12 slides, which sets a pace of about 25 seconds each. No matter what the total duration of the presentation, keeping a steady pace as you advance through the slides ensures that you change what's displayed on screen at regular intervals. This keeps the audience from growing bored by staring at the same image for too long and gives them enough time to properly digest the bite-size chunk of information in each frame.

Three Ground Rules for Storyboarding

Inspired by a Hollywood storyboard, your PowerPoint storyboard helps you manage both the words you speak and the images you show. Follow these three ground rules to keep your storyboard coherent.

1   Keep reviewing the big picture.

2   Maintain a steady pace.

3   Tie your acts and scenes together.

Another way to look at pacing is to think of each frame as a musical beat; your goal is to set a steady beat across the entire storyboard. As you work with the storyboard, think of ways to continue to smooth the flow of frames to make beautiful presentation music. For example, if you've chosen a motif for the presentation, consider how you can weave the theme even more clearly through the headlines at regular intervals.

Rule 3: Tie Your Acts and Scenes Together

One of the big benefits of using the Beyond Bullet Points Story Template is that you can easily see the acts and scenes and how they relate to one another in the Word document. The story template is a particularly effective organizing tool for the Act II scenes, because it shows you a visual hierarchy of your ideas. In each column, you write out the statements in descending order of importance from top to bottom and add additional columns of detail from left to right.

But when you send the story template to the storyboard, you lose the template's ability to show you the hierarchy of your ideas in Act II. Every slide you see in Slide Sorter view looks like it carries the same weight, and each slide follows the next in an equal sequence. You do gain some organizing power by adding hidden storyboard guides for the three acts and three Act II scenes. But because there are so many subpoint slides in a linear sequence, you can easily lose track of how each of these subpoint slides relates to the main point of that Act II scene.

Adding additional hidden storyboard guides, as described in "Tip 2: Scale to Time," later in this chapter, helps you to identify the slides from the 15-Minute Column and 45-Minute Column of Act II so that you can manage them better. But the audience doesn't see the hidden guides, so you should try additional storyboarding techniques to keep the audience focused on the three main ideas in Act II.

For example, when you add graphics to the slides in Chapters 5 and 6, you can integrate the scenes by adding similar graphical elements across each scene or by applying animation techniques across related slides. Pay special attention to the wording of the headlines as you read through them in Slide Sorter view to see whether you can reword them to tie them together more tightly. As you write out the narration in the notes area, you can carry through common themes that you'll later explain with your spoken words.

Whatever techniques you use, regularly return to Slide Sorter view to review all of the acts and scenes to make sure that they tie together.

These three ground rules introduce fundamental ideas that you can explore as you review the storyboard in this chapter and add graphics to it in the next. But now that you have a basic storyboard, you're ready for a rehearsal.

Rehearsing with Your Headlines

Before adding graphics to the slides, which you'll do in Chapters 5 and 6, it's a good idea to rehearse the presentation with only the headlines on the slides.

You might be more comfortable rehearsing alone at this stage, or you could rehearse with your team if you prefer to get some early feedback. To start, find a place to rehearse—either at your desk or in a conference room. In the section "Reading Your PowerPoint Script Aloud," in Chapter 3, you addressed two common problems in public speaking: talking to a piece of paper or a slide instead of an audience, and not being aware of what you're doing with your hands when you speak. Continue to track these issues during rehearsal, but this time, also try to be aware of what you're doing with your body in relation to the computer and the screen.

Stand up to put yourself in a public speaking mode. If you use a remote control device, hold it in the palm of your nondominant hand so that you can advance the slides discreetly. Click **View**, **Slide Show** to begin the presentation. Imagine the audience is in the room, and turn to face them. From the corner of your eye, glance at the first headline that appears on the screen, using it as prompt to remind you about the detailed explanation you wrote in the notes area. When you've nearly finished explaining what you want to say while that slide is displayed, discreetly advance to the next slide while you transition to the next topic with your spoken words, as prompted by the headline on the new slide.

TIP   One of the biggest distractions you can create during a presentation is to return to the keyboard every time you need to advance a slide. This creates a visual distraction, disrupts the natural flow of your delivery, and leaves the impression that the computer is controlling you rather than you controlling the computer. You can free yourself from the computer by using a small remote control device to advance the slides in the presentation. Many of these devices are designed specifically for PowerPoint presentations and attach to a computer using a USB connection with no installation software needed. Some models feature a simple interface with only advance and reverse buttons, and some even include a laser pointer and a button that allows you to black out the screen during the presentation.

Move your body around the room in a natural way when you want to emphasize a point or indicate your enthusiasm. Be aware of where you stand in relation to the screen—avoid being blinded by the light of the projector or standing in front of the projected image. Your goal should be to relate naturally to the audience using your body and voice and to use the screen to complement the presentation, not distract from it. As in the previous rehearsal session, keep your hands at your sides except when you raise one or both of them in a gesture to support an important point.

Rehearsing using only the slide headlines increases your confidence in your topic and ensures that you're comfortable with the pace and flow of ideas. If you're working with a team, it's a great idea to run through a rehearsal like this to review the story, structure, and sequence of the presentation in slide form before proceeding to the design stage.

Now that you have an operational storyboard, here are 10 advanced things you can do with it.

10 Tips for Enhancing Your Storyboard

Your storyboard is a versatile tool to prepare and plan both your spoken words and projected visuals during the presentation. Once you've mastered the basics, try using these 10 tips to enhance the storyboard.

Tip 1: Remind the Audience of Your Purpose

Keep the purpose of the presentation fresh in the minds of the audience by duplicating and redisplaying a key slide in the storyboard.

Click **View**, **Slide Sorter**, and go to Act I, Scenes 3 and 4. Remember, the mismatch between the state of imbalance in Scene 3 and the desired balance in Scene 4 creates the central problem that you propose to solve in the presentation and creates the energy that drives the presentation forward. But as you scroll through the Act II scenes, you might see where people could lose track of the purpose you've established.

To remind the audience of this purpose in Act II, go to Act III, Scene 1 (the crisis), which is the slide on which you summarize the central problem of Act I, Scenes 3 and 4. Select this slide and Press **Ctrl+D** twice to duplicate the slide two times. Drag one copy of this slide to the left of the Act II, Scene 2 storyboard guide, and drag the other copy to the left of the Act II, Scene 3 storyboard guide.

Now after you show the Act II, Scene 1 slides, the duplicated slide briefly reminds the audience of the purpose of the presentation and refreshes your emotional connection with them. The slide will perform the same function after you show the slides of Act II, Scene 2. Besides reminding the audience of your purpose this technique also serves as a visual reminder for you to touch base with the purpose of the presentation as you speak.

Tip 2: Scale to Time

When you read aloud the statements of the story template in "Reading Your PowerPoint Script Aloud," in Chapter 3, you easily scaled down your story without sacrificing its integrity. You did this by omitting the statements in the 45-Minute Column to tell a 15-minute story or by omitting the statements in both the 15-Minute Column and the 45-Minute columns to tell a 5-minute story. You can apply the same technique to the storyboard by creating an extra set of storyboard guides and hiding the unneeded slides.

To indicate the slides created from the 15-Minute Column and 45-Minute Column in the story template, add an additional set of storyboard guides by following these steps.

To create an additional set of storyboard guides

1. Follow steps 1 through 3 in the section "To Create Hidden Storyboard Guides," earlier in this chapter, except type **45 Minutes** in the text box, and change the background color to something that stands out from the other storyboard guides— in this case, dark gray. Make any additional formatting changes you want. (See "Tip 10: Customize Your Storyboard Guides," later in this chapter, for ideas about designing custom storyboard guides.)

2. Click **View**, **Slide Sorter**, select the new slide, and press Ctrl+D eight times to create a total of nine new storyboard guides.

3. Click the first storyboard guide while you hold down Shift, click the last storyboard guide, and then right-click any slide and choose **Hide Slide**.

4. Using the story template as a reference, drag each 45-Minute Column storyboard guide to the left of each series of three 45-Minute Column slides, as shown in Figure 4-19. Review the story template to verify that all of the storyboard guides map back to the correct locations in the PowerPoint storyboard.

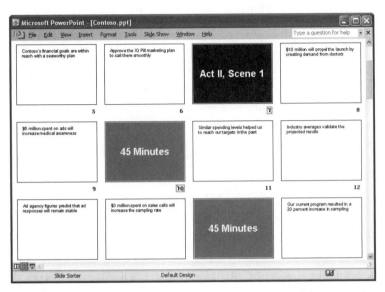

Figure 4-19 *Slide Sorter view, displaying two 45-Minute Column storyboard guides in their proper position.*

Now you can scale the storyboard to time by hiding the slides that you don't need to use in the presentation. If you're creating a 45-minute presentation, do nothing.

To prepare a 15-minute presentation, hide the slides that correspond to the 45-Minute Column in the story template by following these steps.

To prepare a 15-minute presentation

1 Reduce the size of the slides in Slide Sorter view so that you can see all of them at once. In this case, on the **Standard** toolbar, click the **Zoom** drop-down arrow, and click **33%** magnification.

2 Hold down the **Ctrl** key and click the first slide to the right of the first 45-Minute Column storyboard guide and the two slides following, and do the same to select all of the other sets of 45-Minute Column slides.

NOTE Although you can manage the storyboard without them, you can create an additional set of 15-Minute Column storyboard guides if it would be helpful to you to indicate each of the 15-Minute Column slides. To create the storyboard guides, follow steps 1 through 4 in the previous procedure, except type **15 Minutes** in the text box, select a background color different from the other storyboard guides, and position the guides to the left of each slide created from a statement in the 15-Minute Column.

3 With all of the 45-Minute Column slides selected, right-click any slide, and select **Hide Slide**. Now only the 5-Minute Column and 15-Minute Column slides will appear when you give the presentation; the 45-Minute Column slides will be hidden.

To prepare a 5-minute presentation, hide the slides that correspond to the 15-Minute Column and the 45-Minute Column in the story template by following these steps.

To prepare a 5-minute presentation

1 Follow steps 1 and 2 from the previous procedure for a 15-minute presentation.

2 In addition to selecting the three slides to the right of each 45-Minute Column storyboard guide, select the single slides to the left of the 45-Minute Column guides, and then right-click any slide and select **Hide Slide**. Now only the 5-Minute Column slides will appear during the presentation; the rest of the slides are hidden.

Whatever length presentation you give, be sure to run through the slides before the presentation to make certain that you've hidden the correct slides.

When you hide the slides as you scale to time, you maintain a single presentation file that has the flexibility to accommodate different-length presentations without losing the integrity of the story.

REMEMBER When you use the Hide Slide feature, a hidden slide icon containing the slide number is displayed. To reset the hidden slides to be viewed in a slide show, select the hidden slides, right-click any slide, and click Hide Slide again. Keep in mind that hidden slides don't appear on screen when you run a presentation, but they will print unless you clear the Print Hidden Slides check box in the Print dialog box.

Tip 3: Paper Storyboards

When you print the storyboard, you open up multiple ways to see and manage your story. To create a paper storyboard, click **File**, **Print**, and in the **Print** dialog box, click the **Print What** drop-down arrow and select one of the following options:

- Select **Slides** in the **Print What** drop-down list to print an individual copy of each slide that you can tape to a wall or assemble in a loose-leaf notebook that you can flip through as you sketch ideas for individual slides.

- Select **Notes Pages** to print the notes pages and assemble them in a notebook so that you can sketch visuals in the slide areas or take notes to add to the notes areas later.

- Select **Handouts**, click the **Slides per Page** drop-down arrow, and click **1**, **2**, **3**, **4**, **6**, or **9**, to print the corresponding number of slides per page. Printing handouts is a great way to see multiple slides in a single view so that you can focus on improving the flow or sketching out visuals.

Whatever format you choose for the paper storyboards, you should be able to read the headlines clearly so that you can use them as guides to manage the slides. If you make changes to the paper storyboard, be sure to make the corresponding changes to the PowerPoint storyboard.

Tip 4: Nested Storyboards

What if you're not certain which of two stories you want to present until you're standing in front of the audience? "Tip 4: Multiple Stories, Multiple Templates," in Chapter 2, explored the possibilities of developing two related story templates in parallel. Both stories presumably relate to the same topic, so they should share the same Act I, Scene 1 slide (the setting), because this is a general statement about the setting that everyone should agree is true. You can use this single slide as the starting point for whichever story you choose to present from that point forward.

To do this, create a separate PowerPoint file from each story template, and then copy and paste all of the slides from the second presentation to the right of the last slide in the first presentation. This creates a "nested" storyboard in which the second story sits in the same file as the first. Note the number of the slide that begins Act I, Scene 2 of the second story.

When you present Act I, Scene 1, ask the audience a question such as "Which option do you prefer, A or B?" Based on their responses, if you decide to stay on path A with the first story, you advance the slides as usual. But if you decide to take the alternative path B, type the number of the slide from Act I, Scene 2 of the second story and press **Enter** to go directly to that slide and begin that story instead.

The drawback of this approach is that you might have more than a hundred slides in the PowerPoint file to manage, so when you try it out, you'll need to balance the flexibility of a nested storyboard against the management challenges that large storyboards create.

Tip 5: Design for Your Designer

If you're going to work with a professional designer to add graphics to the storyboard in Chapters 5 and 6, you should provide the designer with a completed story template and the formatted storyboard you prepared in this chapter. When you meet with a designer, the story template describes the story and how all of the ideas work together. The storyboard shows the order in which you want the ideas to appear and how you'll reinforce the message through the presentation. Because the designer doesn't have to take on the unnecessary job of figuring out what you want to say and in what order, you'll accelerate the design process and avoid possible confusion. Instead, the designer is freed up to do what a designer does best— designing. Using this approach, you can develop a smooth process that's sure to result in a PowerPoint presentation that gives everyone involved a satisfying communication experience.

Tip 6: Comical Inspiration

It might sound funny at first, but you can learn a great deal about storyboarding by studying comic strips. One of the best books about communicating with a sequence of frames is *Understanding Comics,* by Scott McCloud (Perennial Currents, 1994). Written completely in comic form, McCloud's book is about much more than comics. It begins with a journey through the history of visual communication and ends up reframing your ideas about what you can do with any sequence of frames such as your PowerPoint storyboard. Although McCloud doesn't mention PowerPoint in his book, you can read what he says about the topic in the article *"Understanding PowerPoint: Q&A with Scott McCloud,"* available at *www.sociablemedia.com.*

Tip 7: Customize the Beyond Bullet Points Storyboard Formatter

Many of the features in a conventional PowerPoint design template exist to help you to apply a bullet points approach. These features include a predesigned background that applies to all slides and a default slide layout that places a text box below the title area of each slide and a logo on the Slide Master. Because the Beyond Bullet Points approach uses no bullet points, you configure the slides in a completely different way.

The specific configuration of the Slide Master and Notes Master described in this chapter aligns with a number of research-based principles described in Appendix A. These principles help to ensure that when you add graphics to the slides in Chapters 5 and 6, you'll automatically apply a design approach that helps support effective learning. Key features of the Beyond Bullet Points approach include a blank background on every slide, a default layout with a visual element below the title area, and an optional logo included in the Notes Master.

Instead of setting up the Slide Master and Notes Master every time you send the story template from Word to PowerPoint, you can download and use the Beyond Bullet Points Storyboard Formatter, as described in Appendix B. To avoid problems, don't use a conventional design template for presentations created using the Beyond Bullet Points approach, and don't use the Beyond Bullet Points Storyboard Formatter for presentations created using the bullet points approach.

The Beyond Bullet Points Storyboard Formatter includes all of the formatting changes to the Slide Master and Notes Master described in this chapter. If you want, you can also make the Storyboard Formatter the default so that every presentation you create will be preformatted as a storyboard. In any case, you still need to manually change the layout of all of the slides to a Title and Content format as described in the section, "Changing the Slide Layout," earlier in this chapter.

After you master the fundamentals of the Beyond Bullet Points approach, you can modify the Beyond Bullet Points Storyboard Formatter according to your needs. For example, you might change the font style and color of the title area on the Slide Master or of the notes area on the Notes Master. You might also add a logo, headers, footers, or page numbers to the Notes Master. But before making formatting changes, be sure to review Appendix A to ensure that the changes you make don't throw the presentation out of alignment with the research-based principles that strengthen the Beyond Bullet Points approach.

Tip 8: Notes on Your Notes Pages

When you format the Notes Master according to the instructions in the section "Setting Up the Notes Pages," earlier in this chapter, the Notes Master balances the amount of space on the notes pages equally between the amount of space you dedicate to the slide you show on screen and the amount of space you dedicate to the notes area, which holds the ideas you explain with your voice.

When you add graphics to the slides in Chapters 5 and 6, you can use this view to create a versatile handout for the audience. Removing the line around the slide placeholder, as you did in step 4 of the procedure "To Format the Notes Master," earlier in this chapter, opens up the white space on the printed notes page. The Slide Master and Notes Masters both have white backgrounds, and because neither the slide nor the notes areas will be bounded by lines, the headline of the slide will actually summarize the idea of the entire printed page. To preview how the notes pages will look when printed, click **File**, **Print Preview**, and in the **Print Preview** dialog box, click the **Print What** drop-down arrow and click **Notes Pages**. When you've finished previewing, click **Close** to return to the previous view.

To increase the effectiveness of the notes area, add a subheading to the written notes, as shown earlier in Figure 4-18. In Notes Page view, review the slide headline, think of a few words that add more information to the headline, and then type that text in the notes area. Add boldface formatting to the subheading, and then press **Enter** and begin writing your narration. In the Contoso example, the first headline is *The pharmaceutical industry is navigating a sea of change*. The subheading *An uncertain environment* is helpful because it adds more information and provides a transition from the headline to the text explanation that follows.

Tip 9: Write in Slide Sorter View

When you are working in Slide Sorter view and you want to add text to the notes area of a slide without switching to another view, you can use a little-known feature called Speaker Notes. In Slide Sorter view, click **View**, **Toolbars** and make sure that **Slide Sorter** is selected. Select a slide, and on the **Slide Sorter** toolbar, click the **Notes** button. The **Speaker Notes** dialog box will appear, in which you can enter any text; click **Close** when you've finished. The text you enter in the **Speaker Notes** dialog box will be automatically updated in the notes area of the Normal and Notes Page views of the same slide.

With this handy dialog box, you're free to remain in Slide Sorter view while you manage the slides and add text to any slide you choose.

Tip 10: Customize Your Storyboard Guides

The section "Creating Storyboard Guides," earlier in this chapter, described how to design a basic set of black-and-white storyboard guides. Because these hidden slides won't be seen by the audience, feel free to design them using whatever colors and styles help you to best see the sections of the story in Slide Sorter view. For example, you can make the background red so that the guides really pop out, or you can insert your organization's logo.

When you finalize the design, consider turning the layout into a permanent graphical element so that you don't accidentally change any part of it.

To lock in the design that you use for the storyboard guides so that you don't accidentally make changes to it, make all of the graphical elements on the slide permanent by following these steps.

To turn the layout into a permanent graphical element

1 Follow steps 1 and 2 in the section "To Create Hidden Storyboard Guides," earlier in this chapter.

2 On the **Drawing** toolbar, click the **Rectangle** button, and then drag the sizing handle across the screen so that the **Rectangle** object fills the entire slide. Click the **Fill Color** drop-down arrow, and click a color.

3   Continue with steps 3, 5, and 6 from the earlier procedure, choosing a font color that's visible against the color of the rectangle you selected in step 2.

4   Return to each slide, click **Edit**, **Select All**, and on the **Formatting** toolbar, click the **Cut** icon. Click **Edit**, **Paste Special**, and in the **Paste Special** dialog box, click **Picture (PNG)** or another graphical file format you want and then click **OK**. This transforms all of the elements on the slide into a single, permanent image in the file format you chose. You might need to center the image on the slide.

As with any part of the Beyond Bullet Points approach, feel free to improvise creatively like this once you've mastered the basics.

Chapter 5: **Choosing a Design Style for Your Storyboard**

In this chapter, you will:

1. Clarify your storyboard by adding visuals.

2. Review the three ground rules of designing.

3. Add full-screen photographs and clip art to the slides.

4. Animate selected words from the headlines.

5. Mix and match techniques.

People say a picture is worth a thousand words, but if you're not a professional illustrator where exactly do you get that picture? Turning words into visuals can be a daunting task for anybody, especially if you're used to putting mostly bullet points on your Microsoft Office PowerPoint slides. Fortunately, you've already made your job easier than you might think by using the Beyond Bullet Points approach.

The most difficult job for any designer is usually not the actual design work, but the planning that comes first. Before beginning their creative task, designers struggle to find the answers to a series of questions like: What is the presentation's purpose, and what is a good story structure to apply? What is most important, and where's a good place to begin?

You've already answered these questions and more. In Chapters 2 and 3, you completed the script that serves as the foundation of your presentation, defining its purpose and story structure and establishing the priority and sequence of information. In Chapter 4, you transferred your script to PowerPoint and added the text elements to prepare and plan a new storyboard. Now in Chapters 5 and 6, it's time to add graphics to the storyboard to build an elegant visual structure on top of the foundation you've already created. As you follow the graphic design process in this chapter, you'll start to unlock the visual power of your story.

Designing Using Three Ground Rules

PowerPoint is an easy-to-use and powerful media tool that can produce impressive results. But if you're like most people who use PowerPoint, you're not a graduate of a design school. And in most situations, including the Contoso presentation, you're under a tight deadline and don't have time to take a design course. Fortunately, you don't need design training to produce effective results with your new PowerPoint storyboard. This chapter will introduce and demonstrate a number of basic design techniques that you can start applying to your PowerPoint presentations today.

When you design a presentation, you're planning for a live environment using projected media, spoken words, interaction, printed handouts, and more. Managing such a complex environment can be difficult, so it's important to stay on track using a set of design ground rules.

Rule 1: Design the Complete Experience Around the Headline

The most important thing to keep in mind when you design a PowerPoint presentation is that you're not just designing *slides*; you're designing a complete *experience*. It's easy to

Three Ground Rules for Designing

Your PowerPoint file includes much more than slides; it also helps you plan your spoken words, interaction, handouts, and more. Follow these three ground rules to make sure you design the complete experience:

1. Design the complete experience around the headline.

2. Make your slides collaborative.

3. Try three treatments.

become absorbed in the details of fonts, graphics, and animations on the slides while losing track of your spoken words and how the entire experience helps the audience to understand your message.

To ensure that you properly manage both what you show on screen and what you say with your words, always begin designing the PowerPoint presentation in Notes Page view, as shown in Figure 5-1.

The headline helps the audience to quickly read the main idea at a glance.

A graphical element helps the audience to quickly see what you mean.

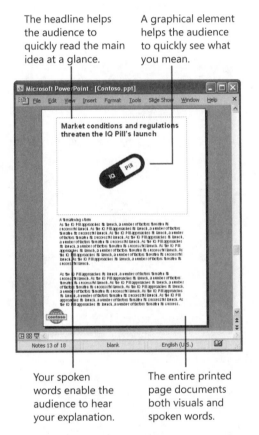

Your spoken words enable the audience to hear your explanation.

The entire printed page documents both visuals and spoken words.

Figure 5-1 *Reviewing both projected visuals and spoken words in Notes Page view.*

To begin designing, click **View**, **Notes Page**, and scroll through all of the slides in the presentation. Starting in this view reinforces the concept that you're designing an experience consisting of both projected visuals and spoken words. As you can see in Figure 5-1, the top half of the page shows what you see on the slide, and the notes area below shows your spoken words. The headline of the slide does double-duty in Notes Page view—not only does it summarize the main idea that will appear on screen during the presentation, but it also summarizes the meaning of the entire notes page.

A valuable byproduct of starting to design in Notes Page view is that at the end of the design process, you have not only well-designed slides but also a useful handout. The composition of this handout is built on three levels of information hierarchy on the page. The top of the hierarchy is the headline, which indicates the meaning of the entire page; the second level of the hierarchy is the visual element, which further explains the headline; and the third level of the hierarchy is the narrative explanation in the notes section, which further explains both the headline and the visual element.

In addition to designing in Notes Page view, you'll work on the PowerPoint storyboard design in Normal view, where you'll compose the graphics on the individual slides, and in Slide Sorter view, where you'll design pacing, flow, and coherence across slides, as summarized here:

- **In Notes Page view**   Design what you say with your spoken words and also what you present on paper.

- **In Normal view**   Design what you present with your projected visuals.

- **In Slide Sorter view**   Design the flow and pacing of the experience.

The Importance of Headlines

Headlines are the cornerstone of the Beyond Bullet Points approach, tying together your story, storyboard, slides, and handouts. The headlines originate as statements in the story template, ensuring that you clearly articulate your ideas to the audience using a persuasive story structure. Sending the statements to the title areas of PowerPoint slides unlocks your ability to create a storyboard of the presentation. You can read the story across the slide titles in Slide Sorter view, and you can write narration related to the headline in the notes area in Notes Page view. When you add graphics to the slides in Normal view, you make sure that the images are simple, clear, and related specifically to the headlines. This keeps the design process focused on effective communication, not on ornamentation or aesthetics. This singular focus on the headline in the Beyond Bullet Points approach ensures that the story stays clear, your spoken words are focused, the visuals are relevant, and the handouts are effective.

As you switch among these views, keep in mind how the different views help you to consider different dimensions of the complete experience.

Rule 2: Make Your Slides Collaborative

If presentations in general didn't require people to actually attend, we could all simply e-mail our documents to one another and save a lot of time. But instead we meet because we find it useful to discuss, collaborate, and make decisions face to face. Your projected visuals can support this sociable nature of meetings by opening up possibilities for collaboration rather than closing them down.

The best way to create engagement is to present only the right information the audience needs to know in the right quantity at the right time. You accomplish this by using the story template to break up your ideas into digestible chunks and then sending those statements to the PowerPoint storyboard, where they become headlines of slides. After you format the Slide Master, you create a consistent and simple layout that serves as the foundation for all of the slides, with a headline at the top and space for a related visual below.

Although the layout for the slides is simple in style, it is sophisticated in its effect. The headline reminds you as a speaker what you want to say while this slide is displayed, and it communicates the topic clearly to the audience. It keeps excess information off the screen and keeps you and your audience focused on a specific topic.

But what might not be evident in the simplicity of this slide is what happens when the audience experiences it along with your verbal explanation. Because the slide design is simple, the audience can quickly scan the headline and visual and understand the idea. Then their attention turns to the place you want it—to *you*, the words you're saying, and the way the information relates to them. Instead of making everything explicit and obvious on the slides, you can leave the slides open to interpretation so that the audience is dependent on you, and you on them.

REMEMBER It might sound counterintuitive, but when you put less information on a slide, you increase the audience's attention because the audience is then dependent on the speaker for explanation, and the speaker is dependent on the audience for feedback.

To assure yourself that you're providing complete information during the presentation, return frequently to Notes Page view during the design process to verify that you explain every slide with your spoken words.

Rule 3: Try Three Treatments

You don't know what you have until you see it, and that's especially true with graphics. That's why you should create a range of options for yourself before you decide what to do with the design of your slides.

When a professional design firm starts a job for a client, it's common practice to present the client with three different design options. From the perspective of the firm, this gives designers a free hand to express their creativity by trying three completely different treatments. From the perspective of clients, this gives a range of options that they can review and select from based on what works for them. From the perspectives of both parties, this provides a way of stepping back from the emotional attachment anyone has to the different designs and gives a point of reference and comparison that can be used in deciding which design direction to take.

This time-tested method will serve you well when you design your PowerPoint storyboard. Select at least three slides from the presentation, and try three completely different design treatments, as described in this chapter. Show the design treatments to your team, and test them on people unfamiliar with the presentation and ask for feedback. When you're satisfied with a design that will work for the audience, extend that design across all of the slides in the presentation. To get started, let's take a look at what you can do with three slides from the Contoso presentation.

NOTE   There are literally endless ways you can apply these three design rules to the slides in the storyboard. This chapter and the next describe a dozen or so options, focusing only on effective and creative things that you can do using graphical elements such as photographs, clip art, and screen shots. All of the examples in these chapters use graphics that can be downloaded free from the Microsoft Office Online Clip Art and Media site, at *office.microsoft.com*.

Applying a Variety of Design Techniques to Three Slides

The sequence of the five scenes of Act I make the first and strongest impression on the audience. As described in the section "Act I: Setting Up Your Story," in Chapter 2, these five brief scenes accomplish the significant and important work of orienting the audience to your story and making the experience personal and relevant to them. Now, when you add graphics to these five scenes in the storyboard, you can powerfully complement the clear and coherent flow of ideas you set in motion in Act I.

You have a lot riding on the first visual impression you make, so look closely at the results of applying different design techniques to the same three slides. To do that, create a new test file that you can use to review the basic design process of the Beyond Bullet Points approach.

Preparing a Test File

It's important to choose a coherent style to apply across the entire presentation, but you can't know what that style will be until you experiment with a few options. To do that, first create a new PowerPoint file that you can use to test your design ideas. Creating a new test file enables you to freely experiment with different design techniques without worrying about making unintended changes to the original file.

To try different design treatments, create a new PowerPoint file with three representative slides from the presentation by following the procedure below.

To create a test file

1   With the PowerPoint file from Chapter 4 open in Slide Sorter view, click **File, Save As**, and in the **Save As** dialog box, enter a new file name that includes *test*—in this case, **Contoso_TEST.ppt**. Click **Save**.

2   Click **Edit, Select All**, and then hold down Ctrl while you click three representative slides from the presentation—in this case, the slides that represent Act I, Scenes 1, 2, and 5. On the **Standard** toolbar, click the **Cut** button, which deletes all of the slides except the three you selected, and then click **Save**.

3   Click **Edit, Select All**, and on the **Standard** toolbar, click **Copy**. Insert the cursor to the right of the last slide, and on the **Standard** toolbar, click the **Paste** button twice. You should now have three sets of three slides each, nine slides in all.

4   On the **Standard** toolbar, click the **Zoom** drop-down arrow, and click a percentage that allows you to see the three slides side by side, as shown in Figure 5-2. You can also click and drag a corner of the PowerPoint window to resize the screen.

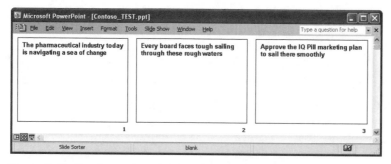

Figure 5-2   *The three selected slides of the test file in Slide Sorter view.*

Beginning the Design Process

Now that you've set up the test file for the three slides, read through the three headlines in Figure 5-2 to remind yourself what you want to communicate over the course of these slides. This chapter describes six design techniques that you can apply to these slides. After you review the range of techniques and are ready to design your presentation, choose three of these techniques to try, or try your own techniques.

To begin designing, go to Notes Page view to review your starting point, as shown in Figure 5-3.

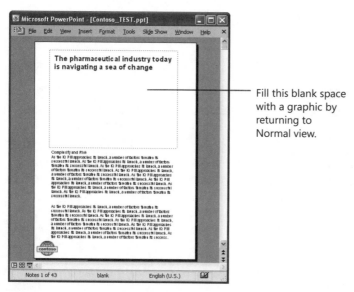

Figure 5-3   *Beginning the design process in Notes Page view.*

In this example of a notes page, you already have a headline in place in the slide area and text narration in the notes area. Your job now is to fill in the blank space between the headline and the notes area with a graphic. To add a graphic, first double-click the slide area to display the slide in Normal view.

Because you already communicate a great deal of meaning with your words, whatever you choose as a graphic for the slide can simply complement the verbal information in the headline and notes area. In the section "Changing Your Slide Layout," in Chapter 4, you applied the Title and Content layout to all of the slides; now each slide appears in Normal view, as shown in Figure 5-4.

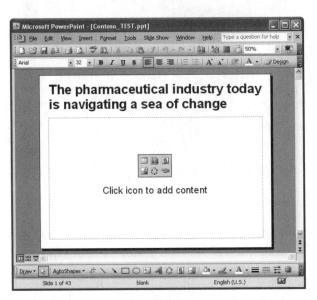

Figure 5-4   *A preformatted slide with the Title and Content layout.*

To add a graphical element to the slide, locate the buttons above the placeholder text *Click icon to add content*; the six buttons are **Insert Table**, **Insert Chart**, **Insert Clip Art**, **Insert Picture**, **Insert Diagram and Organization Chart**, and **Insert Media Clip**. Click the button to insert the type of graphic you want, completing the dialog box if one appears. If you paste a graphic onto the slide without following this procedure, the **Click icon to add content** placeholder will remain on the slide.

You can leave the object in place, because it won't be visible when you run the presentation, or you can right-click it, and on the shortcut menu click **Cut**.

To begin to see the range of visual possibilities for these three example slides from the Contoso presentation, let's take a snapshot of Act I, Scene 1.

Filling the Screen with a Photograph

As you probably remember from the section "Act I: Setting Up Your Story," in Chapter 2, the Act I scenes work their magic by appealing primarily to emotion. One of the most effective ways to enhance their appeal to emotion is by adding a full-screen photograph.

Choosing a Simpler Layout

The Title and Content layout centers the graphic in the middle of the content area below the headline, which works well as a default layout while you master the fundamentals of your new design approach. Some people prefer not to use the Title and Content layout because they find the **Click icon to add content** placeholder distracting. To change the layout of all your slides to a simpler format, in Slide Sorter view, click **Edit, Select All**, click **Format, Slide Layout**, and click the **Title Only** layout to apply it to all of the slides. This creates a default layout of only the title at the top of the slide, and a blank area below. Other advanced layouts and grid options that you can apply are described in "Tip 1: Layouts Beyond the Basics," in Chapter 6.

There are many resources for finding photographs for your presentations. If you're a good photographer, take your own photographs using a digital camera. The Microsoft Clip Art and Media site offers free photographs for download, and some of the stock photography sites license photographs for download at a reduced rate for use in presentations. Your organization might have an in-house photo library you can access. In every case, make sure that you get any permission needed to use the photographs in your presentation.

Remember too from Chapter 2 that a recurring theme, or *motif*, can tie a presentation together, help people relate to what you're saying, and unlock your personality and confidence. You can see the power of a motif come to life when you look for photographs to add to the Scene 1 slide. Because the motif of the Contoso presentation is the sea, start searching for photos using keyword search terms like *sea*, *sailing*, *navigate*, *storm*, *boat*, *rain*, *beach*, or *compass*. A sample search results screen from the Microsoft Clip Art and Media site is shown in Figure 5-5.

This photograph is a nice fit for Scene 1 because it shows the points of a compass, indicating a trip, travel, or a map that the board members might use when they set sail with you on your presentation journey.

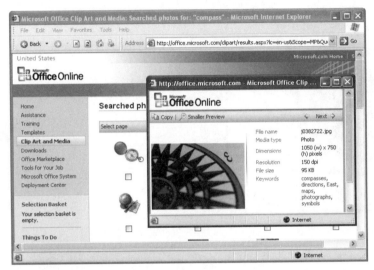

Figure 5-5   *A results page from a search of the Microsoft Clip Art and Media site.*

In most photo databases like the Microsoft site, search results for a particular photograph will include related keyword search terms that can inspire you to search using other terms you hadn't yet considered. When you find a style of photography you like, you might also be able to search for photographs that have related styles.

Whatever photo you choose, you might find that it doesn't fit on the slide the way you want it to or that it is an inappropriate file size for a PowerPoint presentation. To fix these problems, you'll need to apply the three most important techniques you'll use to work with photographs: size, crop, and compress.

When you insert this photograph in the slide, it fills only a portion of the screen, communicating only a portion of its visual potential. To increase its communicative power, resize the photo to fill the entire screen. To do that, click the photo. Sizing handles will appear at each of the four corners and sides of the photo, as shown in Figure 5-6.

REMEMBER The most important techniques you need when working with photographs are size, crop, and compress. To access more photo management features, try using Microsoft Office Picture Manager, which is included with Microsoft Office 2003, or one of the many photo editing software packages on the market, such as Microsoft Digital Image Pro.

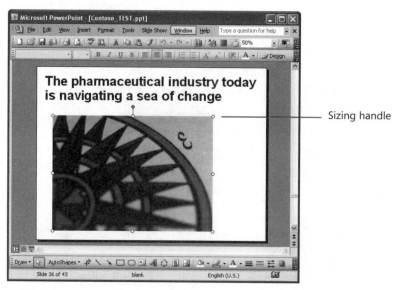

Sizing handle

Figure 5-6   *A selected photograph with one of its sizing handles indicated.*

Hold down the **Shift** key and drag one of the sizing handles to enlarge the photo so that it fills the entire slide area. Holding down the **Shift** key while you drag a sizing handle preserves the proportions of the image as you resize it; otherwise, the photo will be distorted.

Review the picture to make sure that it's crisp and clear at this size. If it isn't, find another image. Never use a photo that is unfocused, grainy, blurry, or otherwise unclear—you'll distract from your message and diminish your credibility as a presenter. People are used to seeing sharply focused photographs in professional media, and if you don't deliver the same in your slides, they'll think less of the presentation, no matter how good the story.

REMEMBER   When you resize a photograph, hold down the **Shift** key while you drag a sizing handle to preserve the proportions of the image.

After you resize the photograph and see that it's clear and focused, you might find that it extends over the edges of the slide. If so, you'll need to crop the image to keep only the portion you want in the slide area. To crop a picture, first display the **Picture** toolbar by clicking **View**, **Toolbars** and selecting **Picture**. Click the photograph, and on the **Picture** toolbar, click the **Crop** button. Cropping handles will appear on the photo, as shown in Figure 5-7. In this example, to crop the right side of the photograph, drag the cropping handle on the right side of the image to the left until the edge of the picture ends at the edge of the slide area.

Cropping Handle

Figure 5-7 *A selected photograph with the* **Picture** *toolbar displayed and cropping handles indicated.*

When the sharp and clear photo completely fills the slide, the last tool to apply is Compress Pictures, a feature available in Microsoft Office PowerPoint 2002 and later. It's not uncommon for a single high-resolution photograph to be hundreds of megabytes in size, unnecessarily bloating the PowerPoint file. This huge image file can create problems when you try to e-mail the PowerPoint file or share it with other people. You can solve this problem before it happens by making sure that the photographs are compressed to the smallest size needed for them to appear clearly on screen.

To compress a photograph, select it and on the **Picture** toolbar, click the **Compress Pictures** button. In the **Compress Pictures** dialog box, click the **Change Resolution** button next to **Web/Screen**. If you want to compress all of the pictures in your presentation at one time, click the **Apply to** button next to **All Pictures in Document.** When you've made your selections, click **OK**. This technique automatically reduces the resolution of photographs to 96 dots per inch (dpi), which ensures that the image is displayed clearly on the screen without taking up too much space in the PowerPoint file.

After you've resized, cropped, and compressed the photograph to fill the entire screen, the next step is to make sure that the audience can read the headline.

Ensuring That the Headline Is Legible

When you insert a photograph in a slide, it might completely cover the headline so that the headline is not visible. To send the photograph to the back of the slide, right-click the picture, and on the shortcut menu, click **Order**, **Send to Back**, as shown in Figure 5-8. This sends the photograph to the back of the slide so that the title area now appears in front of the photograph.

Figure 5-8   *Sending the photograph to the back of the slide makes the headline visible.*

It's important that the headline be clearly visible over the photograph so that audience members at the back of the room can clearly read it. If reading a headline is difficult, as is the case in Figure 5-8, you have a couple of options to make it legible. The first technique to try is changing the font color to something that contrasts with the photograph. Hold down the **Shift** key (to block text editing mode), and click the title area. Click the **Font Color** button on the **Formatting** toolbar, and in the drop-down list, select **White**, or another color that contrasts with the photo. If that doesn't make the headline legible, you can also change the font of the text in the title area to boldface by selecting the title area and clicking the **Bold** button on the **Formatting** toolbar.

If the headline is still not readable, you can clear things up by adding a transparent rectangle below the title area. This rectangle creates contrast between the photograph and the text so that the audience can read the headline more easily.

To make the headline easier to read, create a new rectangle, and apply transparency settings to it by following the procedure below.

To add a transparent rectangle below the title area

1 On the **Drawing** toolbar, click the **Rectangle** button, and click and drag to create a rectangle that covers the entire title area, as shown in Figure 5-9. If you need to resize the rectangle, use the sizing handles to adjust any side or corner.

Figure 5-9 *A new rectangle shape placed over the title area of a slide.*

2 Double-click the rectangle to open the **Format AutoShape** dialog box, and in the **Line** section of the **Colors and Lines** tab, click the **Color** drop-down arrow and click **No line**, as shown in Figure 5-10.

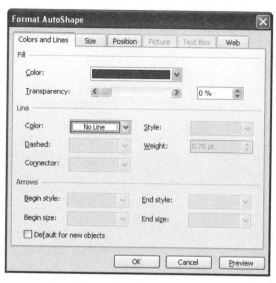

Figure 5-10 *Removing the line from the rectangle by choosing **No Line** from the **Color** drop-down list.*

3 Next, in the **Fill** section, click the **Color** drop-down arrow, click **Fill Effects**, and in the **Fill Effects** dialog box, click the **Gradient** tab. In the **Color** section, select **Two Colors**, and set both **Color 1** and **Color 2** to **Black**. In the **Transparency** section, leave the **From** slider at **0%** and drag the **To** slider to **100%**. In the **Shading Styles** section, click **Vertical**. The **Fill Effects** dialog box should look like Figure 5-11. Click **OK** to close the **Fill Effects** dialog box, and then click **OK** to close the **Format AutoShape** dialog box.

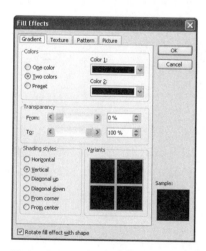

Figure 5-11 *The Fill Effects dialog box, with settings for a gradient rectangle selected.*

4   Right-click the rectangle, and on the shortcut menu, click **Order, Send to Back**. Then right-click the photograph, and on the shortcut menu, click **Order, Send to Back**. The title area should now be in the top layer.

5   The final slide should look similar to the example shown in Figure 5-12.

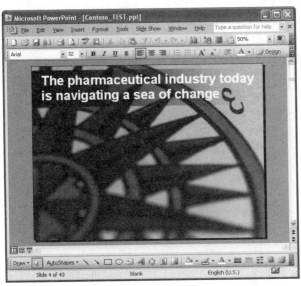

Figure 5-12   *Slide with a gradient rectangle added below the headline to provide contrast.*

The headline in the title area is now clear and readable at the top of the slide. For other photos, you might need to change the color of the rectangle's **Fill Effects** to white instead of black or readjust the rectangle's transparency settings or shading styles to make sure that the text is clear and readable against the specific photograph. When you've finished the first slide, copy and paste the transparent rectangle into the second and third slides and arrange the rectangle as you did on the first slide.

In the completed examples shown in Figure 5-13, the second slide's headline refers to "tough sailing," so a picture of rough water enhances it nicely. In this photo, leaving the title area and transparent rectangle at the top would interfere visually with the wave crest. In a case like this, hold down the **Shift** key as you select both the title area and the rectangle, and drag them to the bottom of the slide. The third headline refers to "smooth sailing," so a picture of calm water works there.

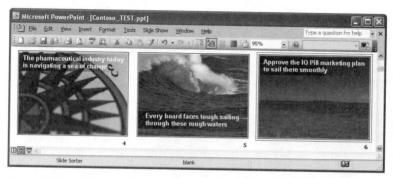

Figure 5-13   *Filling the three test slides with full-screen photographs.*

The combination of headlines and photographs on these slides creates an interesting synergy that enhances the story flow. Any of these photos in isolation might be generic or nondescript, but you've now added a new layer of meaning to the image in the form of the headline. For example, the image of a wave in the second slide might appear anywhere, but when you present it with the headline, you evoke new meaning from it by connecting it with the tough sailing every board must face. Whatever emotional meaning the picture had before, you've now expanded and extended it into the world of ideas, where you have invited the audience to sail the metaphorical waves of your story. This dynamic enhances the connection they have with the story and makes the entire experience striking and memorable.

These three photographs do a nice job of setting the visual stage for your story without distracting from the message, and they also work well together thematically as they flow from one to the next in sequence. There are countless photographs that you could use for this sequence of slides, each with different aesthetics that evoke different emotions in the audience. Aim for simple and elegant photos that reinforce the basic feelings of the slides, and then enhance and amplify those feelings with your spoken words.

After you prepare each slide, check the design in Notes Page view to see how the slide area relates to your spoken script, as shown in Figure 5-14. If you were new to this project and could see only the slide area portion of the presentation, you'd probably think there wasn't much to it beyond a few pictures. But in Notes Page view, you see the context of the slide within the complete presentation experience, narrated by your spoken words.

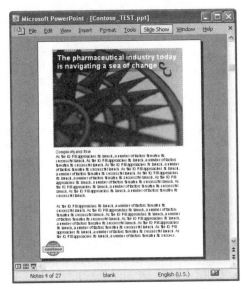

Figure 5-14 *Notes Page view of a slide area, with a full-screen photograph and notes area below.*

The headlines in these example slides do a good job of signaling the ideas of the slides. If you were to hide these headlines, the audience would experience something a little different.

Hiding the Headlines

After you add photographs to the slides, try hiding the headlines to test a new technique. To hide headlines, right-click the photograph on each slide, and on the shortcut menu, click **Order**, **Bring to Front**. Your slides will now appear without headlines, as shown in Figure 5-15.

Figure 5-15 *Three test slides with full-screen photographs and the headlines hidden.*

The headlines that signaled the ideas at hand are no longer visible on these slides to do that. The slides still work, but in a different way. The images continue to signal the motif of the sea, but because they have no headlines, you increase the audience's reliance on you to explain why you are showing these pictures. To use this technique effectively, you would need to become comfortable with the slides so that the photos alone would prompt your memory about what to say next.

TIP   Try hiding the headlines if the visuals alone do a good job of signaling the ideas of the slides and you want to increase the level of visual engagement with the audience. Even if you hide the headlines in a presentation, every slide still maps back to the story structure and sequence you establish in the story template. You need to be comfortable and confident with the story before you use this technique—but it's likely you will be, because you've been working so closely on the story through each step in the Beyond Bullet Points approach.

When you return to Notes Page view, the headlines no longer indicate the main idea of the notes pages. If you print these pages as handouts, the headlines are no longer visible, as shown in Figure 5-16. To make the headlines visible again to help readers quickly understand the idea of each page of the handout, return to Normal view, right-click each photograph, and on the shortcut menu, click **Order, Send to Back**.

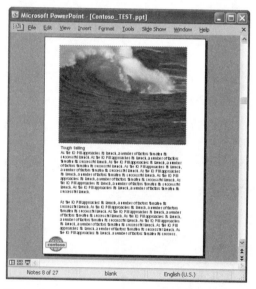

Figure 5-16   *Notes page view of a slide with headline hidden.*

When you use only photographs on the slides, you create a visual trigger that prompts you about what to say and taps into the power of images to open the imagination of your audience. A variation of this technique is to use a visual prop.

Adding a Visual Prop

A classic technique in oral presentations is to hold up a prop and explain how the object relates to the presentation. If you were giving a product demonstration, you would hold up the product and show how it works. If you were giving a general talk, you could hold up any object and improvise on its meaning as you related it to various parts of the story.

You can do something similar in your slides by adding a simple photograph of an object to a slide, as shown in Figure 5-17.

Figure 5-17 *A slide with a visual prop consisting of a simple object against a white background.*

Unlike the photographs of complete seascapes used in the earlier example slides, this photograph shows only an object against a simple white background. A visual prop can be an actual photograph taken against a white background, as in this example, or it can be a *photo object* that has been cut out of a larger photograph and placed against a white background. The emphasis in this type of photograph is completely on the object, displaying it out of its usual context against a white background so that you can use it as a prop.

Although a visual prop is simple, it can produce a sophisticated effect. Again, if you saw this image by itself, you might not think anything of it. But when you add your spoken explanation, you add new meaning to the image. The stark simplicity of an image like this can be quite refreshing and unexpected for audiences that have grown bored with the same generic styles that many organizations use in their visual communications. An added bonus of using a visual prop is that it triggers meaning for you without tying you down. This allows you to improvise more and to come across as more relaxed and authentic, especially if the visual prop is connected to a personal interest of yours.

You can show a visual prop on a slide either with a headline or without. If you choose to hide the headline and the photo fills the entire slide, follow the instructions in the section "Hiding the Headlines," earlier in this chapter. But if the photo is smaller and placed in the center of the white background, there's no full-screen photograph to hide the headline behind. Instead, select the title area, and on the **Formatting** toolbar, click the **Font Color** drop-down arrow and select **White**. This technique makes the white headline invisible against the white background, as was done in Figure 5-17. If you want to create a printed handout, as displayed in Notes Page view in Figure 5-18, you can change the title area of the slide back to black in Normal view.

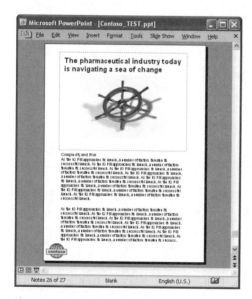

Figure 5-18 *Notes Page view, featuring a slide area with a visual prop, a visible headline, and the notes area below.*

Of course, photographs aren't the only graphical elements in town. Clip art is also a viable option.

Using Clip Art

Although clip art sometimes gets bad press, you can do some effective things with it if you use it well. For example, when you search for clip art in the Microsoft Clip Art and Media site, your results will often produce a piece of clip art described as *Resizable*, as in Figure 5-19. This type of clip art is sometimes called *vector art* in other software applications. The value of this type of graphic is that you can break it into its components and use only a portion of it on a slide. Another advantage of resizable clip art is that you can resize it without ever losing its sharp, clear lines.

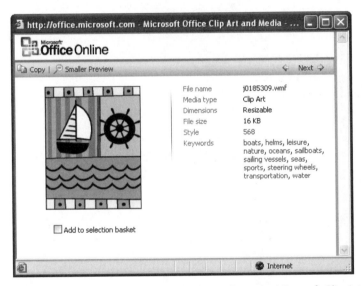

Figure 5-19   *A preview of resizable clip art from the Microsoft Clip Art and Media site.*

You can break apart and resize a piece of resizable clip art without ever leaving PowerPoint, as in the following example from the Contoso presentation. To reuse only certain parts of resizable clip art, break it into its pieces and resize the components you want to use on the slides by following these steps.

To tailor resizable clip art for your slides

1 Copy and paste a resizable clip art graphic into a PowerPoint slide, as shown on the left in Figure 5-20.

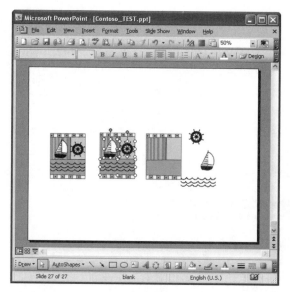

Figure 5-20 *Breaking apart an example of resizable clip art into its components.*

2 Right-click the graphic, and on the shortcut menu, click **Grouping, Ungroup**. (If the **Ungroup** option doesn't appear on this shortcut menu, the clip art is not resizable.) If a Microsoft Office PowerPoint message box appears asking whether you want to convert the graphic to a Microsoft Office Drawing Object, click **Yes**. Right-click the graphic again, and click **Draw, Ungroup** on the shortcut menu. The graphic should be broken up into its component parts, as shown in the middle graphic in Figure 5-20.

3 Select the parts of the graphic that you want to keep, and click and drag these elements away from the rest of the graphic, as shown on the right in Figure 5-20.

4 Copy and paste each of these elements onto the slide areas of each of the three slides.

5 To resize a piece of resizable clip art on a slide, select it to display the sizing handles. Hold down the Shift key, and drag one of the sizing handles to enlarge the graphic to the size you want. (Remember, holding down the Shift key while you drag a sizing handle preserves the proportions of the graphic as you resize it; otherwise, it will be distorted.) The final slides in this example should look similar to Figure 5-21.

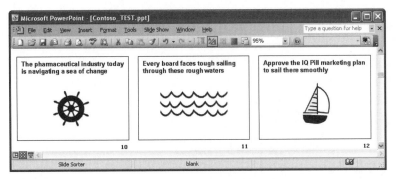

Figure 5-21 *Resizable clip art that has been broken apart, inserted on the three test slides, and resized.*

The three slides with resizable clip art shown in Figure 5-21 are dramatically different from the photographic slides shown in Figures 5-13 and 5-15. Although the clip art doesn't pack the emotional punch of the photos, the slides still work by conveying the bare essence of the topic while relying on you to unpack the message with your spoken words. Looking at these slides in Slide Sorter view demonstrates that using a single style like this helps to keep the visual story consistent across slides.

Like the bare simplicity of the visual props described earlier, the simplicity of the clip art on these slides can be a refreshing change for audiences that are used to sometimes boring or overdesigned visuals. This almost primitive style can create an interesting contrast in the context of a complicated topic and lighten the tone of a meeting. Of course, this style is not for everybody, and as with any design decisions, you should choose only the styles and techniques from the three test treatments that are a good fit with both you and your audience.

If you look at this graphical style in Notes Page view, shown in Figure 5-22, you'll see that even though these graphics are light and simple, they're presented in the context of your spoken words and grounded in the authority you have in the topic.

Photographs, visual props, and clip art present a broad spectrum of visual possibilities, but you can also use words themselves as graphical elements.

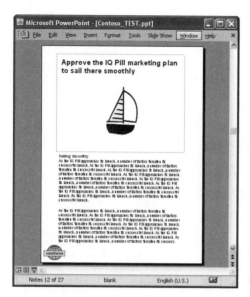

Figure 5-22 *Notes Page view, featuring a slide area with clip art and the notes area below.*

Animating Your Words

For a simple yet sophisticated effect, try turning key words from the headlines into animated graphics on the slides. With this technique, you don't have to spend time searching for ready-made graphics because you create your own.

To create animated words for your slides, add text boxes with a simple animation effect by following these steps.

To create animated words for slides

1 Select the first slide you want to illustrate—in this case, the slide that represents Act I, Scene 1 in the Contoso presentation. In Normal view, click the **Text Box** button on the **Drawing** toolbar. Position the cursor above the middle of the slide and drag it from left to right across the entire screen to draw a text box. Choose a single word or phrase from the headline that communicates a key concept, and type it in this box—in this example, **industry**.

2 Select the text box, and on the **Formatting** toolbar, click **Center**, click the **Font size** drop-down arrow, and select a large font size—in this example, **60**, as shown in Figure 5-23.

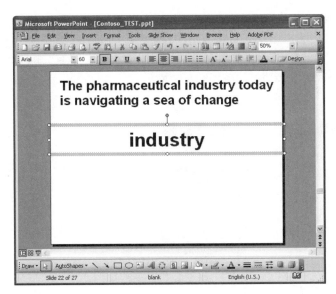

Figure 5-23   *A new text box on the slide, with the word **industry** added.*

3   With the text box still selected, click **Edit**, **Duplicate** to create a second box that has the same formatting. Type another significant word from the headline in this box—in this example, **change**—and then position the text box directly below the first, as shown in Figure 5-24.

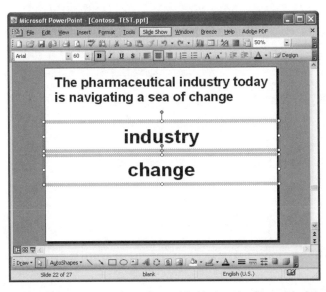

Figure 5-24   *A second text box added below the first, with the word **change** added.*

4 Hold down the Shift key while you select both text boxes, and then click **Slide Show**, **Custom Animation**. In the **Custom Animation** pane, click the **Add Effect** drop-down list, and select **Entrance**, **Fade**. In the **Modify Fade** section, click the arrow to the right of the **Start** button, and in the drop-down list, click **After Previous**. Your screen should look like Figure 5-25.

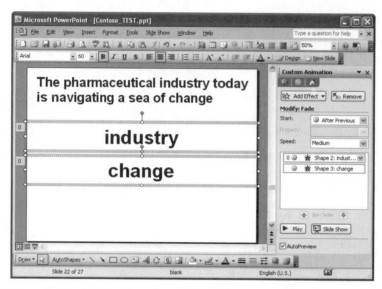

Figure 5-25   *A slide with settings selected to create animated words.*

5 With the two new text boxes still selected, on the **Formatting** toolbar, click the **Font Color** drop-down arrow, and click **White**. Click **Format**, **Background**, and change the background color to **Black**. The slide should look like Figure 5-26.

6 At the bottom of the **Custom Animation** pane, click **Play** to preview the animation effects. When you show this slide during the presentation, the word *industry* will slowly fade into view as you talk about pharmaceutical industry, and then the word *change* will fade in as you talk about navigating a sea of change.

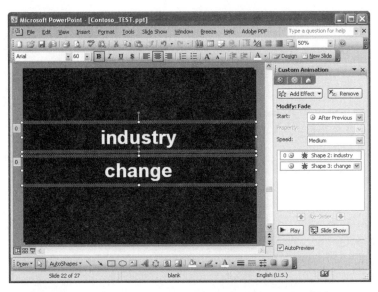

Figure 5-26 *A slide with the animated words technique applied.*

7 Follow the same procedure to add two key words to the second and third slides, as shown in the Slide Sorter view of the three slides in Figure 5-27.

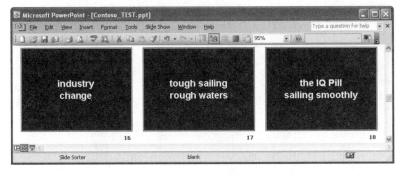

Figure 5-27 *View of the three test slides, with animated words added to each.*

When you show these slides in sequence, they appear to be a single slide with words fading in and out of the screen. This technique creates an interesting dynamic while you speak—when you show only single words or phrases, as in this example, you break the words out of their everyday context and open them up to new meaning. Your audience will then pay close attention to how you'll interpret these words in the context of the presentation.

You can apply many variations to this simple technique. For example, to show only one word or phrase on screen at a time, change the fill color of the text boxes to black, stack them on top of one another, and change the animation effect to start on the next click. For example, on the second slide, the first phrase, *tough sailing*, would fade into the second phrase, *rough waters*, as you talk about the difficult conditions every board faces. Whatever you do, consider how much more visually powerful you've made these slides by eliminating wordy bullet points and stripping down the slides to their essence.

Using the same technique across a sequence of slides ensures a visual consistency that pulls the story forward. And as you can see in Notes Page view, it creates an interesting visual dynamic on a printed page as well. Because the words are actually pulled from the headline and convey the gist of the slide, you could print the notes page with the black background or change it back to white, as shown in the two treatments of the same slide in Figure 5-28.

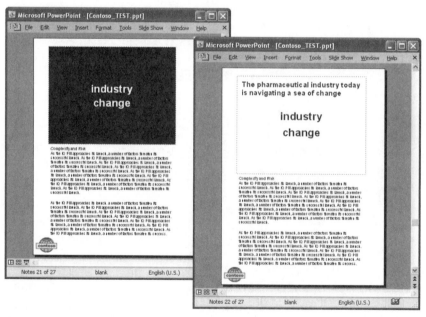

Figure 5-28   *Two views of a notes page featuring animated words in the slide area.*

If you like animating words but also want to include a photographic technique, you can try blending the two together.

Mixing and Matching Techniques

As you explore your graphical options, you can try mixing and matching different techniques to see how they look. For example, you can combine full-screen photographic images, as shown in Figure 5-15, with animated text, as shown in Figure 5-26, to produce an effect similar to Figure 5-29.

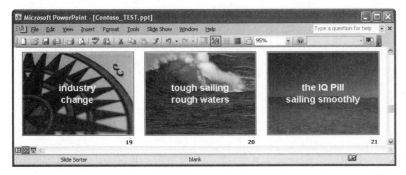

Figure 5-29 *Three test slides with a combination of two techniques: full-slide photographs and animated words.*

In all cases, you should apply the same graphical techniques to a sequence of slides in an act or a scene to help drive the story across the storyboard with a visually consistent style.

Choosing a Style

In your test file, you might have applied three design techniques to the slides based on the suggestions in this chapter, or you might have chosen other techniques of your own. These treatments should be completely different so that you can pick and choose the technique or combination of techniques that makes you comfortable and that connects with the audience.

Review the three treatments that you applied to each set of slides, and show them to other people on your team and gather their opinions. You're certain to get a range of perspectives that will help you to choose the treatments that work best for both you and your audience.

When you choose the style you want, copy and paste the three slides you want to use into the main presentation file, deleting the three slides that you replaced with these newly designed versions. Then apply the new style to the other Act I slides. You should use these newly designed slides as the foundation for the style through you carry through the Act II and III scenes. This ensures that you create a sense of visual continuity.

As you begin to design the rest of your slides, remember to follow the storyboarding ground rules from Chapter 4:

- **Rule 1:** Keep reviewing the big picture.

- **Rule 2:** Maintain a steady pace.

- **Rule 3:** Tie your acts and scenes together.

Because Act II contains a larger number of slides than the Acts I and III, you'll probably need an even broader set of graphical options; these options are described in Chapter 6. But before you move on, review the following 10 tips to whet your creative appetite.

NOTE As you begin to apply the Beyond Bullet Points approach, you can expect that it will take some time to learn and apply the techniques described in this chapter. But as you develop your skills, the process will go faster and your test file will become a handy tool for rapid visual prototyping of creative concepts. As you build presentations over time, you'll develop a personal library of styles that you can review for inspiration on future projects. You should continue to vary the techniques and styles you use to keep things interesting for both the audience and yourself.

10 Tips for Enhancing Your Slides

There are many ways to design your slides building on the foundation of the Beyond Bullet Points approach. Preview these 10 tips to see whether they inspire you to try a range of techniques on your test slides before you pick a style for your presentation.

Tip 1: Composing a Palette

A *palette* is a coordinated range of colors that an artist uses throughout a work. Selecting a palette for your presentation is one of the most effective ways to establish a mood and tone and to create visual consistency across a presentation. In most general graphic design books, you can learn about defining a palette, or you can refer to a book specifically about color, such as *Color Harmony Workbook: A Workbook and Guide to Creative Color Combinations*, by Lesa Sawahata (Rockport Publishers, 2001). When selecting a palette, be aware of the color guidelines your organization might have that relate to branding; these guidelines are usually available from the marketing department. Once you select a palette, you can find instructions for applying it to the presentation in the topic Color Schemes in PowerPoint Help.

Tip 2: Design Inspiration

As you become more comfortable and fluent with the language of design, learn more about basic and advanced design techniques by browsing a newsstand for publications such as *Communication Arts*, *HOW*, or *Computer Arts*; by reading design books such as *Universal Principles of Design*, by William Lidwell, Kritina Holden, and Jill Butler (Rockport Publishers, 2003); or by taking a continuing education course in graphic or broadcast design.

A couple of particularly interesting books that might inspire you are: *Sight, Sound, Motion: Applied Media Aesthetics*, by Herbert Zettl (Wadsworth Publishing, 1998), and *Future Cinema: The Cinematic Imaginary After Film*, edited by Jeffrey Shaw and Peter Weibel (MIT Press, 2003). Although these books are not specifically about PowerPoint, they might stretch you to innovate the traditional presentation experience using experimental media techniques and technologies.

SEE ALSO For a steady supply of PowerPoint-related design inspiration, go to the Beyond Bullets blog, at www.beyondbullets.com, and read the many articles and interviews available at the Sociable Media Web site, at www.sociablemedia.com.

As you explore the range of design resources, always keep in mind that the special requirements of the presentation environment call for you to design not just your projected visuals, but also your spoken words, handouts, and other environmental elements. You'll explore how all of these elements can work together in Chapter 7.

Tip 3: Storyboard Sketchpads

Sometimes paper simply works better than a computer screen—that is, if you like to sketch with a pencil. Instead of beginning the design process on your computer, try printing the storyboard and sketching the visuals for slides by hand. Follow the instructions in "Tip 3: Paper Storyboards," in Chapter 4, and print a copy of the storyboard in whatever format works best for you. Grab a pencil and sketch an idea for the visual of each slide. Try to complete sketches for all of the slides before you return to your computer to find visuals to match the sketches. Creating sketches of the slides first can accelerate the design process because it keeps you from getting distracted among the many visual possibilities you'll find when you search through photo and graphics libraries. A series of sketches can also help you to select a consistent style, because you see all of the slides together in the printed pages and can consider a design for all of the slides at once.

Tip 4: Savvy Simplicity

Sometimes choosing a simple look or an unpolished style can be a savvy and sophisticated strategy. If everyone presents the same slick, polished, and flawless style, everyone's presentations will look the same. If you choose something simple to contrast with the norm, you'll make a memorable impression. This is a strategic decision based on what you want to accomplish. Always make choices that make you comfortable when you present and that express something of your own character and personality.

Tip 5: Sail Through a Single Photograph

Here's an advanced technique that you could apply to the five slides of Act I of the Contoso presentation: Insert the same photograph of the sea on all five slides. Show only the sea in Scene 1, add a sailboat to the sea in Scene 2, add a storm cloud on the horizon in Scene 3, add an island with a palm tree in Scene 4, and add a screen shot of the marketing plan projected on the sail of the sailboat in Scene 5. When you show the slides in sequence, they'll appear as a single frame with animation.

Tip 6: A PowerPoint Design Library

If you have colleagues who are also using the Beyond Bullet Points approach, consider pooling your resources to create a PowerPoint design library. If your organization uses Microsoft SharePoint, you could use it to create a collaborative Web site for people who are willing to share their PowerPoint files. For example, you could create folders labeled *Photographic Techniques*, *Clip Art Techniques*, and *Animated Word Techniques*. Anyone who created a presentation using one of those design techniques would then post it in the corresponding folder. You and the members of your team would no longer have to begin presentations from scratch; instead, you'd have a library of ideas ready for you to check out.

Tip 7: Inspiration as Big as a Billboard

If you're looking to jump-start your creative engine, look no further than right outside your windshield. That's exactly where some interesting creative concepts loom high and wide across your view—in the form of very large visuals called billboards. A well-designed billboard will catch your eye, communicate some information, make you smile, and prompt you to act. That sounds like decent credentials for any PowerPoint slide too, so be on the lookout when you're searching for new creative ideas. Just be sure to stay within the constraints of the three design ground rules established in this chapter so that your PowerPoint slides always stay directed to your primary goal: effective communication.

Tip 8: The Subtlety of Animation

As a general rule, keep animations subtle and simple, and add them only when they enhance a specific point you want to reinforce. For example, as you advance to a new slide, you can add a subtle Fade animation to the graphical element as the slide appears. In the clip art example shown in the three slides of Figure 5-21, the wheel could turn slightly, the three lines that represent the waves could appear in sequence, and the sailboat could move from left to right. Introducing a small degree of movement on screen maintains the audience's interest without distracting from your message. For more information about PowerPoint's animation features, visit the PowerPoint Help files.

Tip 9: Making the Transition

You can add a single, subtle transition to all of the slides to maintain consistent movement between slides, but be careful not to distract the audience with unnecessary movement in the presentation. You can do this in Slide Sorter view by clicking **Edit**, **Select All** and then clicking **Slide Show**, **Slide Transition**. In the **Slide Transition** pane in the **Apply to Selected Slides** section, select a subtle transition such as **Fade Smoothly** or **Fade Through Black** to apply it. In the **Modify Transition** section next to **Speed**, click a speed in the drop-down list. In the **Advance Slide** section, select the **On Mouse Click** check box if you want to advance the slide manually. Whatever transition you choose, the most important criterion is that people remember the *message* of the slides and not the movement between them.

Tip 10: More Graphical Resources

If you're looking for graphical resources beyond the Microsoft Clip Art and Gallery site, many resources are available online. Visit Corbis, at *www.corbis.com*, to preview an online photo database; the company offers special subscriptions priced for PowerPoint users. Hemera also has an online photo database, at *www.hemera.com*, as well as packages of the photo objects and resizable (vector) clip art described in this chapter. Other photo databases include Getty Images, at *www.gettyimages.com*, and Stock.XCHNG, a free stock photo site, at *www.sxc.hu*.

Chapter 6: **Expanding Your Graphical Options**

In this chapter, you will:

1. **Add screen shots to slides.**

2. **Explain an idea over several slides by using a diagram.**

3. **Explore ways to display quantitative information.**

4. **Reinforce the three main points in Act II.**

5. **Experiment with advanced design techniques.**

Any of the techniques described in Chapter 5 might work in Act II on a single slide or across a sequence of slides. But because you have a larger number of Act II slides, you'll need an even wider range of graphical options.

Act II of the story template shifts from an appeal to emotion to an appeal to reason. You can enhance your appeal to reason with a range of evidence, including quantitative data, case studies, anecdotes, research reports, and surveys. You can also supplement your ideas with a range of graphical elements, including diagrams, charts, and even video clips. As with the graphical techniques you've applied so far, anything you choose here as a graphic should be simple and always map back to the specific meaning you describe in a slide's headline.

One of the simplest and most overlooked sources for graphics for Act II is your computer screen.

Snapping a Screen Shot

When you're looking for a visual to explain the headline of a slide, consider a screen shot. Almost anything that can be viewed on a computer screen can also be displayed on a Microsoft Office PowerPoint slide, including pictures of your desktop, Web pages, documents, and more. To create a shot of your screen, you can simply press **Print Screen** and then, in PowerPoint, click **Edit**, **Paste** to paste the image on the slide. Commercial screen shot programs allow you many options for customizing your shots, including adding a drop shadow, as in the image of the Microsoft Office Online Clip Art and Media site, shown in Figure 6-1.

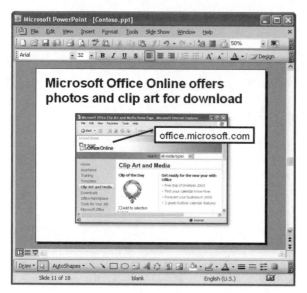

TIP   A label was added to the slide shown in Figure 6-1 giving the Web page address so that the audience can make a note of it. You can add a label to any graphic on a slide to clarify your main point. To add a label, on the **Drawing** toolbar, click **AutoShapes, Callouts**, and then click the style you want. After you add the label to the slide, you can modify it by adding text and adjusting the formatting as you would with any PowerPoint AutoShape.

Figure 6-1   *Slide with a screen shot of the Microsoft Clip Art and Media site, with a label added that indicates the Web address.*

Depending on how you create the screen shot, you might need to resize, crop, and compress it using the same techniques you used in the section "Filling the Screen with a Photograph," in Chapter 5. In Figure 6-1, the screen shot simply shows a Web page, without presenting the actual details of the text on that page. If you do want to show the details of a screen shot, crop out everything that's not essential to the idea and make sure that the portion of the image that contains the details is large enough to be read by people at the back of the room.

One particularly effective way to use a screen shot is to manage the way you present detailed information.

Displaying Detailed Numbers

When you make a presentation, you don't have to limit yourself to showing information exclusively on a slide; you can use other techniques to convey data that you can coordinate with your projected visuals. For example, in Act II, Scenes 2 and 3 of the Contoso presentation, a number of headlines present a dollar figure indicating the amount you plan to spend on a particular activity—for instance, *$10 million spent on sponsorships will increase visibility*.

Each dollar amount or other piece of quantitative information included in a headline is likely derived from a Microsoft Excel spreadsheet or another data source that reflects the detailed analysis that produced it. You could probably spend an hour discussing the details of any single figure, but if you did that, you wouldn't have time to cover any of the other points in the presentation.

To avoid getting bogged down during a presentation, bring printouts of the spreadsheet providing the detailed financial analysis and explanation that back up the headline. Then create a screen shot of the actual spreadsheet, and add it as the visual element of the slide, as shown in Figure 6-2.

SEE ALSO If you get a detailed question about quantitative data during a presentation, answer it quickly if you can. Otherwise, graciously defer the question to a later time—to either the Q&A session or another date, if appropriate. As you'll see in the section "Handling Q&A," in Chapter 7, one of the main goals in the Beyond Bullet Points approach is to structure a story that anticipates and answers many of the questions the audience might have. But even if you get feedback from the audience during the presentation indicating that you missed a question, it's important to avoid veering off track to keep you story from unraveling, as described in "Keeping Control of Your Story," also in Chapter 7.

Now the headline communicates the main idea that you want to get across, and the tightly cropped screen shot of the spreadsheet indicates that you can back up your point, without showing the detailed numbers. When you display this slide, tell the audience that the information is backed up by the spreadsheet printout and that you'd be happy to review and discuss the details after the presentation.

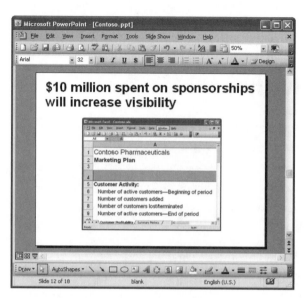

Figure 6-2   *A slide with a close-up screen shot of an Excel spreadsheet.*

By using the slide to indicate that you have information available in another form, you're using PowerPoint as a tool to manage what's happening on-screen and off-screen as well. As always, the headlines of the slides should establish the idea you want to communicate at any and every point in the presentation.

In addition to using screen shots, you can use diagrams to show people what you mean.

NOTE A projected screen is limited in its ability to show detailed information in a way that everyone in the room can understand. The fine print is usually not visible to people at the back of the room, and the audience might be overwhelmed by too much information on one slide. Instead, use your slides to provide an overview of the information, and provide the details in a handout that allows the audience to see the complete source of the data, its context, and the analysis behind the numbers.

Explaining an Idea Using a Diagram

A diagram is an effective tool to illustrate a process or how the parts of something relate to the whole. You can use diagrams in two ways: to explain an idea across several slides or to explain an idea on a single slide. The technique you use depends on the amount of time you can spend on your explanation.

For example, you can use a diagram to explain the section of Act II, Scene 2 of the Contoso story template shown in Figure 6-3 in two ways, depending on whether you make a presentation that lasts 45 minutes or 15 minutes.

15-Minute Column: How?	45-Minute Column: Why?
$25 million spent on TV ads will increase consumer awareness	The plan's first phase will generate awareness in the LA market
	The second phase quickly expands into the New York market
	The third phase launches the program nationally and in Europe

Figure 6-3 *An example of 15-Minute and 45-Minute Columns in Act II, Scene 2 of the Contoso story template.*

If you had only 15 minutes for the presentation, you'd display only the slide with the 15-Minute Column statement, which reads, *$25 million spent on TV ads will increase consumer awareness*, as shown in Figure 6-4. Based on the pacing for a 15-minute presentation, you'd spend about 40 seconds on this slide, as described in "Reading Your PowerPoint Script Aloud," in Chapter 3.

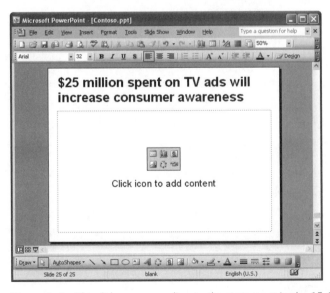

Figure 6-4 *The slide corresponding to the statement in the 15-Minute Column in Act II, Scene 2.*

If you had 45 minutes for the entire presentation, you'd display not only the 15-Minute Column slide in Figure 6-4, but also the three slides that correspond to the next level of detail in the 45-Minute Column, as shown in Figure 6-5. The headlines of these three 45-Minute Column slides read across: *The plan's first phase will generate awareness in the LA market*; *The second phase quickly expands into the New York market*; and *The third phase launches the program nationally and in Europe*.

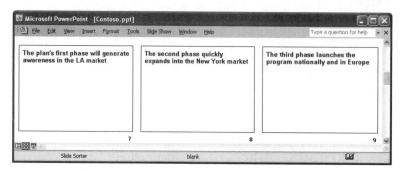

Figure 6-5   *The slides corresponding to the 45-Minute Column in Act II, Scene 2.*

The pacing for a 45-minute presentation is about 1 minute per slide. In this example, you'd spend a minute explaining the 15-Minute Column statement and then a minute on each of the three 45-Minute Column statements, for a total of 4 minutes on the four slides related to this idea. Because you have more time to explain the idea in the longer presentation, you could use a single diagram broken apart across this sequence of 45-Minute Column slides.

To create a diagram for the three slides, read the headlines in Slide Sorter view, as shown in Figure 6-5. Determine which type of diagram would be best to explain the idea. In this case, the headlines describe the three phases of a plan, so a linear process diagram is a good fit. To create a linear process diagram, double-click the last slide in the sequence to display it in Normal view.

Creating a Diagram

When you're choosing a diagram format, a good place to start looking is the predesigned diagrams provided with PowerPoint. To view the predesigned diagrams, click the **Insert Diagram and Organization Chart** button, located above the *Click icon to add content* placeholder. If you find a diagram that you want to use in the **Diagram Gallery** dialog box that appears, click it and then click **OK**. You can edit this diagram just like any other AutoShape in PowerPoint.

If you don't find what you're looking for in the **Diagram Gallery** dialog box, you can create your own diagram. For example, to describe the three-step process in the three headlines in Figure 6-5, you can create a process diagram using PowerPoint's AutoShapes by following these steps.

To build a basic diagram using PowerPoint AutoShapes

1 Right-click the **Click icon to add content** object, and on the shortcut menu, click **Cut**. On the **Drawing** toolbar, click **AutoShapes,** and scroll through the categories of AutoShapes in the drop-down list to find the shape you need. In the example in Figure 6-6, **AutoShapes**, **Block Arrows**, **Chevron** is selected.

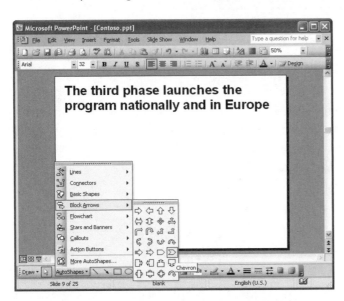

Figure 6-6   *Selecting an arrow AutoShape.*

2 Click and drag across the right side of the screen to draw the arrow, as shown in Figure 6-7. If you need to resize it, click and drag one of the sizing handles.

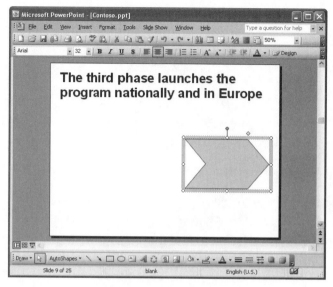

Figure 6-7 *Drawing an arrow AutoShape.*

3 Select the AutoShape, and type a label—in this case, **phase 3.** Select the
AutoShape, and on the **Formatting** toolbar, click the **Font Color** drop-down arrow
and select white. Click **Align Right**, click **Bold**, then click **Increase Font Size** as
many times as necessary to get the font size you want—in this case, the final size
is **36**. The arrow should look similar to the example shown in Figure 6-8.

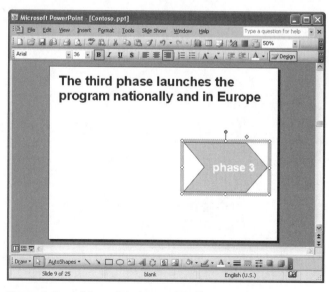

Figure 6-8 *Adding a label to an AutoShape.*

4   Double-click the AutoShape, and in the **AutoShape** dialog box, select the **Colors and Lines** tab. In the **Fill** section, click the **Color** drop-down arrow and select black, and in the **Line** section, change the **Weight** setting to **5 pt**. The dialog box should now look similar to Figure 6-9. Click **OK**.

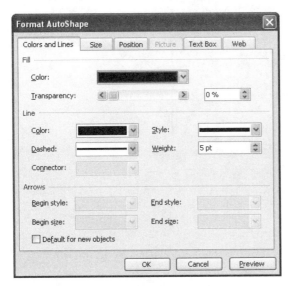

Figure 6-9   *Formatting an AutoShape.*

5   Right-click the AutoShape, and on the shortcut menu, click **Copy**. Then right-click the slide, and click **Paste**. Select the new AutoShape, and drag it to the left of the first AutoShape, as shown in Figure 6-10. Select the second AutoShape, and edit the label—in this case, change it to **phase 2**. Then select the AutoShape, and on the **Drawing** toolbar, click the **Fill Color** drop-down arrow and select a new color—in this case, dark gray.

6   Right-click the second AutoShape, and on the shortcut menu, click **Copy**. Then right-click the slide, and click **Paste**. Select the new AutoShape, and drag it to the left of the second one. Select the new AutoShape, and edit the label—in this case, change it to **phase 1**. Then select the AutoShape, and on the **Drawing** toolbar, click the **Fill Color** drop-down arrow and select a new color—in this case, light gray.

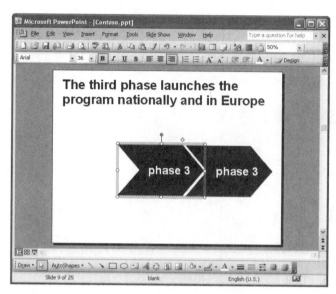

Figure 6-10   *Adding a second AutoShape.*

7 Drag the three AutoShapes on the slide to the approximate position you want. Hold down the **Shift** key while you click the three AutoShapes, and then on the **Drawing** toolbar, click **Draw, Align or Distribute, Align Middle**, and then click **Draw, Align or Distribute, Distribute Horizontally**. Click a blank area of the slide to deselect the AutoShapes; the final screen should look similar to Figure 6-11.

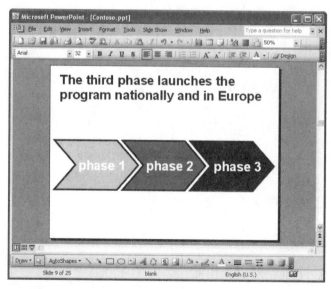

Figure 6-11   *A diagram with formatting applied.*

Explaining an Idea Across Three Slides Using a Diagram

Now view the completed diagram in the context of the other two slides in the sequence in the Contoso story example, as shown in Figure 6-12.

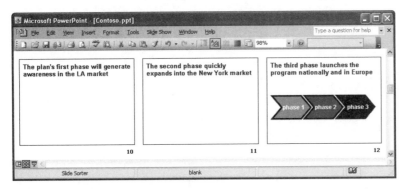

Figure 6-12 *The three related slides, with the third slide containing a diagram.*

Think of these slides as a filmstrip with three frames, each of which describes a single phase. To use the diagram in the preceding two slides, copy and paste the completed diagram into slides, deleting components that have not yet been explained, by following these steps.

To build a diagram to explain an idea across three slides

1 Double-click the slide in the third position, which contains the completed diagram, to display it in Normal view. Hold down the Shift key and select the three AutoShapes that form the diagram, and then right-click an AutoShape, and on the shortcut menu, click **Copy**.

2 Scroll to the slide in the second position, right-click the slide, and on the shortcut menu, click **Paste**. Right-click the *phase 3* AutoShape, and on the shortcut menu, click **Cut**. Hold down the Shift key and select the two AutoShapes on the slide, and then right-click an AutoShape, and on the shortcut menu, click **Copy**.

3 Scroll to the slide in the first position, right-click the slide, and on the shortcut menu, click **Paste**. Right-click the *phase 2* AutoShape, and on the shortcut menu, click **Cut**. The final three slides displayed in Slide Sorter view are shown in Figure 6-13.

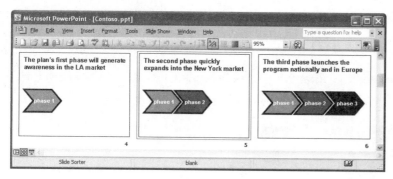

Figure 6-13 *A diagram explained across three slides.*

When you show these three slides in sequence, the audience sees what appears to be a single slide with animation. But as the presenter, you know that this is actually a sequence of three slides, with each slide representing a frame of the animation. Returning to Notes Page view, shown in Figure 6-14, you can see that the first frame in the sequence is described in the notes area; the next two phases will be described on separate notes pages. For more information about how this approach differs from conventional animation and how it aligns with related research, see "Tip 2: Unconventional Animation," later in this chapter.

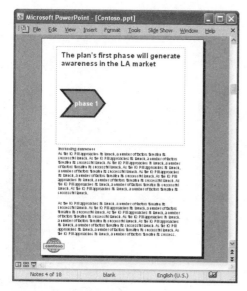

Figure 6-14 *Notes Page view, containing one section of the diagram in the slide area and the corresponding narration in the notes area.*

Using this approach ensures that you always link the idea you show on a slide with the verbal explanation contained in the notes area. This keeps you from overwhelming the audience with too much information at one time, which can shut down their ability to digest it. Instead you present the information in measured amounts at an even pace as you gradually build up the meaning of the diagram to its completion.

Explaining an Idea on a Single Slide Using a Diagram

If you use a diagram to explain an idea across three slides, as shown in Figure 6-13, what should you put on the slide that shows the 15-minute statement that precedes these three slides? You have at least two options, depending on the length of the presentation. If you know you're giving a 45-minute presentation, on the 15-minute slide, you could include a screen shot of an Excel spreadsheet, as was done earlier in Figure 6-2, but in this case referring to the detailed spreadsheet that explains the $25 million to be spent on television advertising.

Or, if you know you have only 15 minutes for the presentation, on this slide you could show the complete diagram you created, shown earlier in Figure 6-11. The diagram is simple enough that you can quickly summarize the idea of the slide with the 40 seconds you have available, reviewing the three phases of the advertising campaign. You could animate the diagram on the single slide by applying the built-in animation features within PowerPoint, but because you have only 40 seconds to spend on the slide, animation might not be necessary.

Explaining an idea with a diagram is effective; using a chart is another option.

Explaining an Idea Across Slides Using a Chart

A chart is one of the most common ways to illustrate quantitative information in a graphical form on a PowerPoint slide. If the best way to illustrate a *sequence* of related headlines is by using a single chart with animation, you can do so by applying a technique similar to explaining an idea across slides using a diagram. With the sequence of headlines in place in the storyboard, you'll know exactly what you want to communicate before you start building the chart.

For example, the series of 45-Minute Column headlines from Act II, Scene 2 of the Contoso story template describes the results of a trial advertising campaign, as shown in Figure 6-15. Based on the pacing for a 45-minute presentation, you'd spend about 1 minute explaining each statement.

15-Minute Column: How?	45-Minute Column: Why?
$15 million spent on other ads will increase awareness online and off	A trial ad campaign found 20 percent response rate to the IQ Pill name alone
	Adding the tagline "smart thinking" increased response rate 10 percent
	Adding the tagline "twice as smart" increased response rate 25 percent

Figure 6-15   *A single idea explained by three statements in Act II, Scene 2 of the Contoso story template.*

These three headlines shown in Slide Sorter view in Figure 6-16 state that *A trial ad campaign found 20 percent response rate to IQ Pill name alone*, but *Adding the tagline "smart thinking" increased response rate 10 percent*, and *Adding the tagline "twice as smart" increased response rate 25 percent*. It would be helpful for the board to compare the response rates by seeing them together in a single graphic— in this instance, a bar chart would do the job.

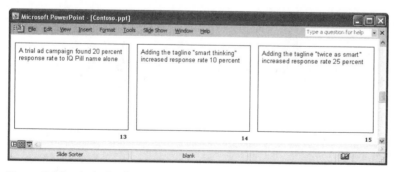

Figure 6-16   *A single idea explained by three headlines in Act II, Scene 2 of the Contoso story template.*

To explain the results of the Contoso ad campaign in this example, you can build a bar chart and describe it over the three slides.

To explain an idea across a sequence of slides using a chart, create the chart and adjust it for each slide of the sequence by following these steps.

To build a sequence of slides that use a chart

1 Double-click the slide in the third position to display it in Normal view. Click the **Insert Chart** button, located in the *Click icon to add content* placeholder, as shown in Figure 6-17.

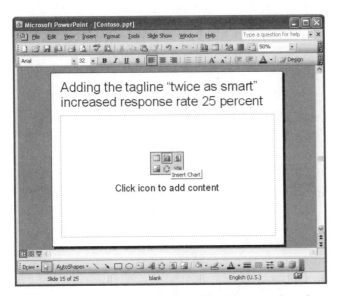

Figure 6-17   *A slide with the **Insert Chart** button selected.*

2 A chart will be automatically inserted into the slide. Edit the chart data source as you normally would. Keep the design of the chart simple, as in the example chart shown in Figure 6-18. (Formatting charts can be a detailed process; for general guidelines on chart design; see "Tip 6: Show Me the Numbers," later in this chapter.) Right-click the chart, and on the shortcut menu, click **Copy**.

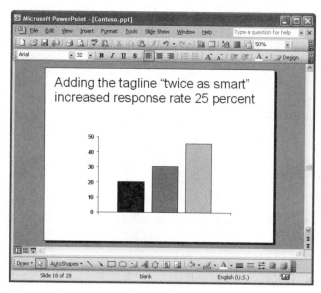

Figure 6-18   *A simple chart inserted in the slide.*

3   Scroll to the slide in the second position, right-click the slide, and on the shortcut menu, click **Paste**. Right-click the chart, and click **Grouping, Ungroup** on the shortcut menu. A message box will appear, asking whether you want to convert the chart to a Microsoft Office drawing object, as shown in Figure 6-19. Click **Yes** to perform the conversion.

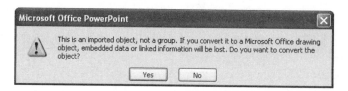

Figure 6-19   *A message box asking whether you want to convert the chart to a drawing object.*

4   Right-click the chart, and click **Grouping, Ungroup** again to break the chart into its components, as shown in Figure 6-20.

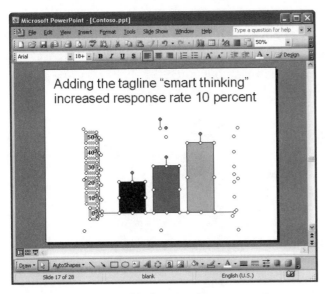

Figure 6-20 *Breaking the chart into its components.*

5 Select and delete the chart elements that don't apply to this slide—in this case, the third bar. The slide should now look similar to Figure 6-21. Right-click any element of the chart, and on the shortcut menu, click **Regroup**. Right-click the chart, and on the shortcut menu, click **Copy**.

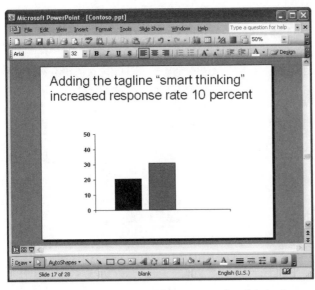

Figure 6-21 *Removing chart elements on the slide in the second position.*

6   Scroll to the slide in the first position. Right-click the slide, and on the shortcut menu, click **Paste**. Right-click the chart, and on the shortcut menu, click **Ungroup**. Select and delete the chart elements that don't apply on this slide—in this case, the second bar. The slide should now look similar to Figure 6-22. Right-click any part of the chart, and on the shortcut menu, click **Regroup**.

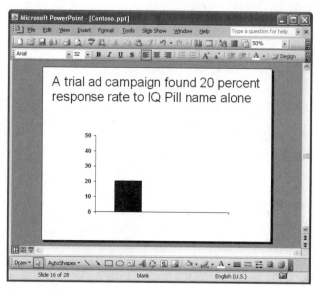

Figure 6-22   *Removing chart elements on the slide in the first position.*

In Slide Sorter view, the final chart sequence should look like the example shown in Figure 6-23. If the chart in the third position is linked to a datasheet within PowerPoint or to an Excel spreadsheet, when you update the data, you'll need to return to the slides in the second and first positions to update them manually.

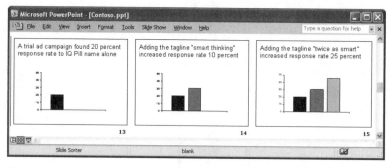

Figure 6-23   *A chart explained across three slides.*

When you explain the chart to the audience over the sequence of slides, it appears to them to be a single slide with animation. But as the presenter, you know that these are really three slides, each of which is linked to the notes area, as you can see in the Notes Page view of the second slide, shown in Figure 6-24. This approach ensures that each specific action in the animated sequence maps back to the spoken words contained in the notes area. To read about research related to this technique, see Appendix A.

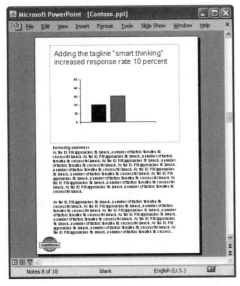

Figure 6-24 *Notes Page view, containing one section of the chart in the slide area and the corresponding narration in the notes area.*

As in the diagram example, if you know that you have only 15 minutes for the presentation, on the 15-Minute Column slide, you could show the complete chart you created, shown earlier in Figure 6-18. The chart is simple enough that you can quickly summarize the idea of the slide in the 40 seconds you have available. You could animate the chart on the single slide by applying the built-in animation features within PowerPoint, but because your time is limited, animation might not be necessary.

Now that you've expanded the range of graphical options a bit, it's time to return to the storyboard to see how you can start improving the story as a whole.

Improving Your Storyboard

When you prepared and planned the storyboard in Chapter 4, you added new slides and reviewed ways to reinforce the flow and pacing of the slides. Now you can build on that foundation by adding some visuals to key slides in the presentation.

Adding Graphics to the Title and Closing Credits

In a Hollywood film, the opening title sequence establishes the mood and tone of the story to come. You can achieve a similar effect by adding graphics to the title slide. In the section "Adding a Title and Closing Credits," in Chapter 4, you created the title slide by duplicating the slide with the Act III, Scene 3 statement and placing it to the left of the first slide in the presentation. You then added the story template title and byline as the subhead, as shown in Figure 6-25. In the Contoso example, the full title reads: *Charting the course to marketing results with the IQ Pill: Contoso Marketing Presentation by Pat Coleman.*

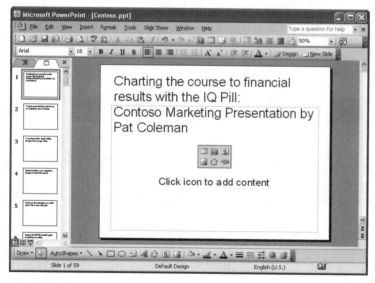

Figure 6-25   *Title slide created in Chapter 4.*

Apply the same style to the title slide that you did to the other slides in Act I. For example, if you use the photographic design technique for the Act I slides, you could use the same style for the title slide, as shown in Figure 6-26.

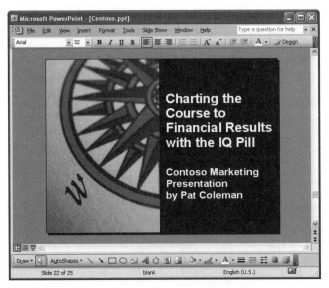

Figure 6-26 *Title slides with photographic style applied.*

This slide was built by adding a single graphical element: a photograph from the Microsoft Clip Art and Media site inserted in the left half of the slide. In addition, the slide background color was changed to black and the title area font color was changed to white. The font size was adjusted and the title capitalized, and the text box was then moved to the right.

Apply the same technique you apply to the title slide to the closing slide, adding a simple image or a line of text that you want the audience to remember after the presentation. As noted in Chapter 4, this slide might include your organization's name, your contact information, a Web address, or a simple image that conveys the theme of the presentation.

Reinforcing the Three Main Ideas

Chapter 4 stressed the importance of tying together the acts and scenes in the storyboard, and a set of strong visuals can help you to do the job. In this section, you'll develop the three main ideas from the 5-Minute Column of the story template, which are the backbone of your reasoning in Act II.

In Slide Sorter view, hold down **Ctrl** while you select the three slides containing the 5-Minute Column statements, and then right-click one of the slides, and click **Copy**. Open the test file you created in Chapter 5, position the cursor after the last slide, and then right-click and click **Paste**. Consider ways that you can enhance these three important slides with a consistent design treatment so that when the audience sees them, they'll know that you've reached an important point in the presentation.

For example, Figure 6-27 shows three slides that state the three main ideas of the Contoso presentation. A single new graphical element has been added to each of these slides—again, photographs from the Microsoft Clip Art and Media site.

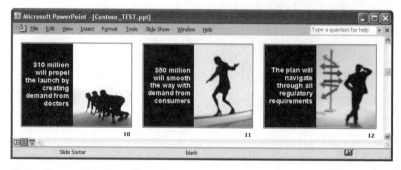

Figure 6-27   *The three slides that introduce the major scenes in Act II of the Contoso storyboard, each with the same graphical style applied.*

Each photo was inserted, resized, cropped, and positioned in the right half of each slide, and the slide background was changed to black. The title area font color was changed to white, the text box was narrowed, and the alignment of the text was changed to align to the right. Because these photos have the same style, they present an especially distinctive impression that drives the story visually through Act II.

As you can see in Figure 6-28, these slides look distinctive in Notes Page view as well.

NOTE   You might notice that the photographs used in this example appear out of focus, which violates the directive to always use sharply focused photographs given in "Filling Screens with Photographs," in Chapter 5. In this case, however, the photographs were created with a blurry style to produce an intentional artistic effect. Once you've mastered the basics of designing slides, you have room for interpretation, as long as your choices don't distract from your message and your story stays clear and understandable to your audience.

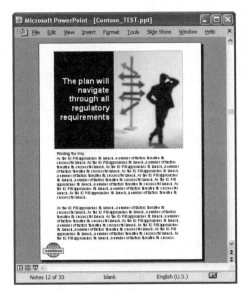

Figure 6-28 *Notes Page view, showing how a distinctive look is carried from Normal view to Notes Page view.*

You can try a similar coordinated visual treatment within the scenes of Act II, or you can change the background color of all of the slides in a scene, as described in "Tip 3: Color-Coded Slides," later in this chapter.

Aligning with the Research

It's easy for any designer to become absorbed in the creative possibilities of a project and lose sight of the audience. To make sure that your design stays focused on helping the audience understand what you intend to communicate, it's a good idea to learn some of the basics of the science behind effective learning with multimedia. Educational psychologist Richard E. Mayer and others have developed a set of research-based principles that can keep the design process grounded in the most recent scientific understanding of how the mind works. Some of these principles and related resources are described in Appendix A. You'll find that the Beyond Bullet Points approach aligns with much of this research and sets the stage for you to continue to refine your work as you learn more about it.

Rehearsing the Presentation

After you design the first draft of the storyboard, you now have all of the basic components of the presentation, so try a rehearsal. Stand next to your desk or in a conference room, and rehearse the presentation while you advance the slides. In the section "Reading Your PowerPoint Script Aloud," in Chapter 3, you addressed the need to look at the audience and to be conscious of what you're doing with your hands. In the section "Rehearsing with Your Headlines," in Chapter 4, you learned to pay attention to what you do with your body and how you relate to the screen. During this rehearsal, be conscious of your voice and facial expressions.

During a presentation, all eyes are on you, and people will watch for cues that indicate your enthusiasm and interest in a topic. If you speak in a monotone and appear disinterested, you shouldn't be surprised if the audience mirrors your lack of enthusiasm. Instead, vary your voice to emphasize important points, and pause for effect when you want a particular point to sink in. You've been working hard on your story; let your enthusiasm come through your voice, as well as your facial expressions.

As you rehearse, you're sure to run into rough spots or things that you want to change in the presentation, so keep a piece of paper handy for jotting down revision notes to yourself as you go. Then return to the presentation to make any final changes to the slides.

Finalizing the Notes Pages

When you finish adding graphics to all the slides, return once again to Notes Page view to review the notes areas and make sure that your written words are clear and concise. Begin with the first notes page: read the headline, review the visual, and then read the notes area to make sure that everything flows smoothly. When you've read the last line in the notes area, scroll down to the next notes page and make sure that it reads smoothly as a continuation of the story from the previous notes page. It's a good idea to print the entire document as notes pages at this point so that you can check the wording and flow.

Getting Clearance and Approvals

Now that you've reviewed the complete presentation, you should get any necessary clearance and approval you might need for the information you'll present. This is especially important in the Contoso scenario because the presentation relates to the pharmaceutical industry, as it would be in other highly regulated industry such as finance or research. In any case, it's always a good idea to have someone with fresh eyes take a look at the presentation to verify that you didn't miss anything, make a typographical error, or misstate something. When you prepare the presentation for review, plan to send it as notes pages so that it can be cleared not only for what appears on screen, but also for the information covered in the notes area. You can send the review copies as printed notes pages or in an Adobe Acrobat PDF file, as described in the section "Sending Your Notes Pages (Not Your Slides)," in Chapter 7.

Congratulations on completing your PowerPoint storyboard! In Chapter 7, you'll move on to the third and final step of the Beyond Bullet Points approach, producing your script. Before you do that, take a look at these 10 tips for improving on the basic techniques described in this chapter.

10 Tips for Enhancing Your Slides

You've got a solid start on the basic possibilities for designing the storyboard, and you can now continue to expand your skills and develop your approach. These 10 tips offer advanced ways you can improve on your design.

Tip 1: Layouts Beyond the Basics

You can keep your graphic design consistent by coloring inside the lines. Professional designers rely on a system of grids to help guide them in their layouts. These grids ensure a consistent layout structure throughout a presentation, manage the important balance between white space and the graphical and text elements on slides, and prevent visuals from being positioned too close to the border of a screen.

You began designing with a basic slide layout consisting of a headline at the top and a visual centered in the area below. But when you hide the headlines or start moving visual elements around, you need to adopt a consistent layout structure to remove the distractions that a cluttered or an unharmonious layout would present.

If you plan advanced layouts, either work with a designer to develop a grid or review one of the many books on designing grid systems. Because slides are projected on a screen, film or broadcast layout books such as *The Visual Story: Seeing the Structure of Film, TV, and New Media*, by Bruce Block (Focal Press, 2001), are helpful. Because notes pages can be printed, print layout books such as *Editing by Design: For Designers, Art Directors, and Editors—The Classic Guide to Winning Readers*, by Jan V. White (Allworth Press, 2003), can be useful. General layout books such as *Grid Systems in Graphic Design*, by Josef Muller-Brockmann (Arthur Niggli, 1996), can help as well. The difficult challenge of designing a layout system for PowerPoint presentations is to find a single, elegant approach that works effectively for both projected slides and printed notes pages.

Once you decide on a layout system, you have a couple of options in PowerPoint that can help you to apply it. The easiest technique is to use PowerPoint's built-in Grid and Guides features. In Normal view, click **View**, **Grid and Guides**. In the **Grid and Guides** dialog box, in the **Grid Settings** section, click a setting in the **Spacing** drop-down list and select the **Display Grid on Screen** check box, and then click **OK**. Alternatively, in the **Guide Settings** section, select the **Display Drawing Guides on Screen** check box to display guides that you can use to customize your own temporary grid. Search PowerPoint Help for more information about using grids and guides.

Tip 2: Unconventional Animation

A simple diagram or chart can effectively illustrate the headline of a single slide. But a common problem in PowerPoint presentations is that the diagram or chart is too complex to be understood—or at least not understood all at once on a single slide. You address the underlying root of this problem by breaking down the ideas in the story template into smaller chunks, as in the 15-Minute Column and 45-Minute Column statements from Act II, Scene 2 of the Contoso story template, shown earlier in Figures 6-3 and 6-15. When you send these statements to PowerPoint, each statement becomes the headline of a slide to create three related slides you present in the same sequence as the story template. You then fully describe the details of each phase in the notes area of each slide.

This technique is different from conventional animation techniques in which all animation occurs on a single slide. Instead, you explain information only in the chunks that are mapped to the headlines across a series of slides. This technique ensures that you present information evenly over the sequence of the explanation, showing only the correct information at the correct time. To read more about research related to this technique, see Appendix A. If you find that your headlines don't quite map to the sequence in which you want to present information, return to the story template and adjust the statements there first, and then return to PowerPoint to edit the headlines accordingly.

Tip 3: Color-Coded Slides

Filmmakers use a number of techniques to keep scenes varied and interesting without losing the consistency of message that comes from a strong story. One of these techniques is to design a set or scenery with a coordinated palette. You can do something similar by adding some color to the Act II slides and scenes. Try this technique by changing the background color of the three slides containing the 5-Minute Column statements from Act II of the story template. These three slides were described in the section "Reinforcing the Three Main Ideas," earlier in this chapter, and shown in Figure 6-27.

To color-code these slides in Slide Sorter view, click the slide that contains the first main idea, and then hold down **Ctrl** and select the slides that contain the second and third main ideas. Now right-click one of the slides, click **Background** on the shortcut menu, and in the **Background** dialog box, click the **Color** drop-down arrow, select a color, and then click **Apply**. This changes the background color of each slide to the color you choose. As you display slides in the presentation, the change in color in each of

> **TIP**   Rather than change background colors, another related color alternative is to choose a different font color for all of the headlines within each Act II scene. Changing only the font color of the headlines is not as dramatic as changing the background color, but it still helps to tie each scene together in a subtle way.

these slides indicates that you have made a transition to a new topic; which should also be reinforced by your spoken words.

Another technique is to change the background of all of the slides of each Act II scene. To do this, select the first slide of Act II, Scene 1, and then hold down **Shift** while you click the last slide in that scene. Right-click one of the slides, click **Background** on the shortcut menu, and in the **Background** dialog box, click the **Color** drop-down arrow, click a color, and then click **Apply**. Now all the slides for this scene are the same color, which indicates to the audience that these slides are all part of the same scene. This technique also helps you to manage the scenes in the storyboard in Slide Sorter view because you can now see each scene clearly distinguished from the others by color.

Tip 4: The Split Screen

Try doubling your impact by splitting the screen. In the section "Act I, Scene 4: Aiming for Balance," in Chapter 2, you explored the energizing force that defines the problem between Scenes 3 and 4 in Act I. You can magnify this energy and keep it flowing through the presentation by creating a slide that reinforces the problem-solution focus of the story and inserting it at several key points in the presentation.

To build a split screen in the Contoso example, locate the Act I, Scene 3 slide that reads, *Market conditions and regulations threaten the IQ Pill's launch.* In Normal view, add a black rectangle that fills half the screen vertically. Click the title area, change the font color to white, and send the title area to the back to hide it. Add a graphic of a pill from the Microsoft Clip Art and Media site, add a text box, and type the text **IQ Pill** in the box.

Next copy and paste the pill and the black rectangle onto the next slide. The headline of the Scene 4 slide reads: *Contoso's financial goals are within reach with a seaworthy plan.* To create your own graphic, insert a text box on the right in this slide. Type a dollar sign in the text box, increase its font size to 208 points, and change the font color to white. Click the title area, change the font color to white, and send the title area to the back to hide it. In Slide Sorter view, the two slides should look similar to Figure 6-29.

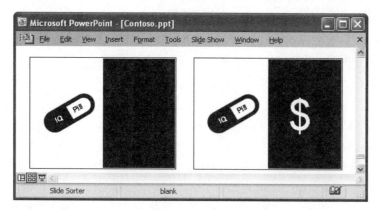

Figure 6-29 *Sequence of two slides using a split-screen technique.*

Now when you show the Scene 3 slide, the pill will appear as you begin to narrate the slide using the corresponding notes area. When you advance to the Scene 4 slide, the dollar sign will seem to appear on the same slide as you begin narrating that slide. When the audience members see these two images contrasted side-by-side and listen to your description, they'll be struck by the imagery.

To keep the image fresh through the presentation, in Slide Sorter view, select the Scene 4 slide, click **Edit**, **Duplicate** twice, and then click and drag the copies to the left of the first slides of Act II, Scenes 2 and 3. When these slides appear in these positions during the presentation, you can say something like "You might recall that the IQ Pill's launch is threatened by market conditions and regulations, but Contoso's financial goals are within reach with a seaworthy strategy. Here's the next part of that strategy." When the audience sees this same slide again at these later points in the presentation and hears your explanation, it will refresh the purpose of the presentation and keep the audience emotionally involved.

In the Notes Page view of the Scene 4 slide, shown in Figure 6-30, showing the title area on the slide doesn't work because it would interfere significantly with the layout, so you would need to make sure that you emphasize the meaning of the slide in the written notes below. You also might need to add a border to the slide area, as in this example, so the white half of the image appears bounded by a line. This isn't the perfect solution, but as with the entire design process, you'll need to constantly balance different elements to find the best solution for any particular context.

TIP   This split-screen technique also works well when you place two contrasting photographs in juxtaposition. Here one photograph might show the state of imbalance in Scene 3 contrasted with a photograph of the desired balance of Scene 4, revealing the purpose of the presentation through your spoken words and this contrast of images.

Tip 5: Visual Rhetoric

One interesting source of inspiration for your design is the field of *visual rhetoric*, which explores the ways that images are used to persuade in fields such as advertising. Just as advertising is a source of inspiration for story structure, as described in "Tip 8: The Story of Advertising" in Chapter 2, it's also a treasure-trove of inspiration for creative visual techniques for presentations. Start paying attention to the way advertisers use color, photographs, layouts, and other techniques to catch your attention, tell a story, and persuade. If you dig into the techniques of well-designed ads, you might uncover some valuable tips that you can apply to your PowerPoint presentations.

Figure 6-30 *Notes Page view, including a slide area with a split-screen technique applied.*

Tip 6: Show Me the Numbers

Although many of the guidelines and much of the writing and research related to charts deals with displaying them on paper, PowerPoint charts are usually projected on a wall with a live presenter explaining them. Because there is the added element of verbal explanation in the live presentation environment, charts designed on a slide can generally be simpler than those displayed on paper without a live presenter. With the Beyond Bullet Points approach, you're always certain that the chart on the slide area is always fully explained by the headline and the notes area, as you can see in Notes Page view. Displaying the chart over a series of slides that are mapped to a sequence of headlines, as described earlier in this chapter, helps to introduce the information in chunks at an appropriate pace for the audience to understand.

To keep a chart free of clutter and focused on the data at hand, simplify its formatting by removing excess lines, graphical treatments, colors, and grids. Avoid adding unnecessary ornamentation or special effects because doing so can inhibit the audience's ability to understand it. For research related to this topic, see Appendix A. Strive for a minimalist style that will allow the numbers to speak for themselves.

When you need to show your numbers using a chart, consider consulting one of the many books that can help you to display data effectively, including *Show Me the Numbers: Designing Tables and Graphs to Enlighten*, by Stephen Few (Analytics Press, 2004).

Tip 7: A Diagram and Chart Library

Many individuals and organizations use a relatively limited range of PowerPoint diagrams and charts to explain the information that relates to their work. Instead of formatting diagrams and charts from scratch every time, it's a good idea to design a single set of commonly used graphics that carry a clear and consistent design according to the best design principles described in "Tip 6: Show Me the Numbers." You can then use Microsoft SharePoint to create a central site to store the PowerPoint files, as described in the section, "Tip 6: A PowerPoint Design Library," in Chapter 5. Whether you design the set of charts yourself or hire a professional information designer to help, standardizing the way you display quantitative information can both save you time formatting and ensure that you maintain the integrity of the data you display.

Tip 8: Working with Designers

If you have the resources, invite a professional designer to help you design your slides and storyboard. Bring the designer in early—if possible, while you write the story template—so that the designer can absorb and learn from your thinking process. If you can't bring a designer in early, at least have the story template and storyboard prepared before your first meeting, as described in "Tip 5: Design for Your Designer," in Chapter 4. That way, you'll have a solid starting point that will enable you to take the basic techniques of this chapter to the next level.

Always walk through the slides in Notes Page view with the designer to make sure that he or she can see the relationship between the projected image on screen and your spoken words. Spend time talking through the animated sequences of slides if you plan to use diagrams and charts. When everyone is on the same page, ask the designer to provide you with three completely different visual treatments of key slides in a test file that you select from Acts I and II. Then you can compare the treatments and choose the elements and styles that are the best fit with you and your audience. Ask a lot of questions to be sure that you understand why the designer is proposing a particular treatment. Through your interaction, you're sure to spark new creativity and understanding that will set the stage for a well-designed presentation.

Tip 9: The PowerPoint Triptych

A variation on the technique described in the section "Reinforcing the Three Main Ideas," earlier in this chapter, is to create a *triptych*, or a single slide with three vertical graphical elements placed side-by-side. To create a triptych, review the three main points of Act II, represented by the 5-Minute Column statements in the story template. Find three vertical photographs, photo objects, or pieces of clip art that convey each of the ideas, and then insert them on a single slide. Resize and crop them as needed so that they fill three equal vertical spaces on the slide.

Position this slide as the first slide of Act II, Scene 3. Duplicate the slide twice, and on one copy, delete the first graphic; this slide goes in the position of the first slide of Act II, Scene 2. On the other copy, delete the first and second graphics; this slide goes in the position of the first slide of Act II, Scene 1. When you show these three slides in these positions in the presentation, you will appear to be building a three-panel slide whose three parts are completely assembled in Act II, Scene 3. By reinforcing the three main ideas of your presentation with a triptych, you can triple the power of your Act II message.

Tip 10: Unified Design

The Beyond Bullet Points approach offers a unified design approach that results in a single PowerPoint file that works well across projector, paper, and browser. You accomplish this by starting to design in the most challenging view—Notes Page. When you take the complete media experience into account and balance projected images with spoken words, you produce a document that works as a printed handout and also as a package that you can convert to an online presentation with little additional work, as described in the section "Producing an Online Presentation," in Chapter 7. If you have a good story to tell, why not tell it through as many different media as possible?

Chapter 7: **Bringing Your Story to Life**

In this chapter, you will:

1. **Remove distractions from the presentation environment.**

2. **Rehearse the delivery of the presentation.**

3. **Develop a dialog with your audience.**

4. **Try advanced presentation techniques.**

5. **Deliver a dynamic presentation using Microsoft Office PowerPoint.**

The root of the word *inspire* means "to breathe," and that's the ultimate objective of the Beyond Bullet Points approach—to inspire you with the confidence and tools you need to breathe deeply and relax more when you present.

Although the slides of the Contoso presentation look dramatically different than they did originally, the real fruit of your labor is your confident understanding of what you want to say and how you want to say it. You have expanded PowerPoint's capability beyond a tool for designing slides into a tool that helps you to think clearly, organize your ideas, structure a story, and express yourself with a limitless range of media possibilities. When you open the completed PowerPoint file, you actually have a sophisticated media toolkit that blends your clear story with the delivery technology.

Now it's time to use that toolkit to bring your story to life.

Producing Using Three Ground Rules

In Hollywood, the term *production* refers to the point when filmmakers capture the live action of actors on film. Film directors spend a great deal of time setting up scenes and filming the action many times so that they'll be able to use the best performances in the final cut. But you don't have that luxury in your PowerPoint production because you're presenting in a live environment, which means that you typically get only a single shot at engaging the audience.

Managing the complex mix of elements in a live presentation can be challenging, but you already have firm control over the projected media, spoken words, and printed handouts in the form of your PowerPoint file. As you use the PowerPoint file to produce the presentation, a set of ground rules can help keep the presentation experience in balance.

Rule 1: Make Your Media Transparent

It's easy to lose your focus on the message when there are endless things you could do to fine-tune the PowerPoint file, such as adding more graphical elements, animations, and special effects. One of the major advantages of keeping the basic format of the slides simple, which you did in Chapters 4 through 6, is that a simple design keeps you from being distracted by unnecessary details and the audience from being distracted by too much happening on the screen. Removing distractions leaves you in control of the media instead of the media controlling you.

You use PowerPoint well when people don't even notice you use PowerPoint at all. The last thing you want is for someone to compliment you on your slides—that would mean that the medium called attention to itself instead of your ideas. The most important outcome of the presentation is that the audience understands the meaning you intend to communicate. When you finish the presentation, you want the audience to talk about your special ideas, not your special effects.

Making your media transparent can be a challenge. But just as you work hard to make the story structure invisible within the flow of the story, you also need to work hard to make sure that the other elements of the production are invisible too. That means removing distractions from the entire live presentation experience, beginning when the audience walks into the room and ending when they leave it.

> ## Three Ground Rules for Producing
>
> Your PowerPoint file helps you manage your spoken words, projected visuals, and printed handouts. Follow these three ground rules to ensure that the rest of the live presentation experience is engaging:
>
> 1 Make your media transparent.
>
> 2 Create a dialog with your audience.
>
> 3 Improvise within constraints.

Rule 2: Create a Dialog with Your Audience

A good way to look at a presentation is as a dialog in which the audience grants you permission to speak first. While you deliver the presentation, you're the only one speaking, so you start the dialog at an intellectual level. You end the presentation at an interpersonal level, when the audience gets to speak too.

You establish the topic of the dialog when you set up the story in Act I of the story template. You present your intellectual arguments by specifying the audience as the protagonist of the story, answering the clarifying questions that every audience will wonder, and defining the core problem that the audience wants to solve. In Act II, you present the reasons why the audience should accept your solution, anticipating their questions as you explain why and how your reasoning is sound.

Finally, in Act III, the audience can respond at an interpersonal level, asking you questions and eventually deciding whether to accept your recommendation to do or think something new.

Keeping this model of a dialog in mind, continue to think of ways to make the presentation experience more engaging and interactive both at the intellectual level of your story and at the interpersonal level, where you invite the audience to participate in the dialog. For example, to increase engagement at an intellectual level, invest plenty of time on focusing and refining the story template to make sure that it directly addresses the audience's concerns and anticipates any questions they might have about your reasoning. And when you transfer the story to PowerPoint, choose a simple design for the slides that increases the reliance of the audience on you to explain the slides within the context of the story.

To increase engagement at an interpersonal level, try some of the techniques in the section "Developing a Dialog," later in this chapter, such as asking the audience questions or opening the floor to Q & A.

Rule 3: Improvise Within Constraints

It's important to align your PowerPoint presentation with your unique personality so that you make an authentic connection with the audience. For example, when you choose a motif for the presentation that's related to a personal interest, your enthusiasm will emerge when you speak. And when you spend the time to carefully plan the presentation, you develop a deep confidence in your story that frees you to improvise from the slides instead of being chained to reading bullet points. All this leads to a more relaxed and comfortable approach that will make the audience feel more relaxed and comfortable too.

A presentation is not a free-for-all, however, so it's important to improvise within the constraints of a specified form. This fundamental principle is applied in many arts, including jazz, in which musicians improvise only after they've mastered the fundamental techniques of the musical form. You can improvise on the constraints defined in the ground rules presented throughout this book once you've mastered the basic presentation forms.

Removing Distractions

Up to now, this book has concentrated on helping you to prepare a PowerPoint file that minimizes distractions. You remove unnecessary information from the presentation by narrowing the focus of the story template. You keep extraneous information out of the slide area by following the storyboard and design ground rules. And you keep both graphics and words focused on the headlines. Now that you've removed distractions from the PowerPoint file, it's time to focus on removing distractions from the environment in which you'll present it.

Preparing the Environment

The physical environment in which you present is just as important as the story you tell. The quality of your hard work is diminished if the room is physically uncomfortable, if there are distracting noises, if you don't have an electrical outlet within reach of the projector, or if the room looks just plain shabby. Just as you have a personal responsibility for the story template, you also have a personal responsibility for the physical experience of the environment in which you present. You'll need to use your leadership and diplomacy skills to work with facilities managers or meeting planners to ensure that everything is in order.

If you have access to the room where you'll present, visit it in advance of the presentation so that you can plan for your needs. In the Contoso presentation, for example, you should reserve the board room for at least an hour a couple of days in advance. When you visit the room, you can review the options for configuring the physical space, and you can also rehearse the presentation in the actual environment. If you're not able to visit the physical location in advance, contact someone familiar with the room to find out about the room setup.

TIP   Lighting the room properly for a PowerPoint presentation can be a challenge. On the one hand, you want people to see the screen clearly, but on the other hand, you don't want the room to be so dark that people start to doze off. Some of the latest models of data projectors have brighter displays that allow the audience to see the images on the screen clearly without turning down the room lights. When you visit the room where you'll present, try out the projector and stand at the back of the room to review things from the perspective of audience members sitting there. Adjust the lighting so that everyone in the room can see the slides and see you clearly too. You might need to ask a facilities manager to help if the lighting controls are not readily accessible or if you need additional lighting.

At a minimum, both you and your audience should be physically comfortable in the environment. You should have a base of operations when you present, such as a podium, and have the physical freedom to move around the room comfortably as you speak.

When you're comfortable with the physical environment, turn to the technology you'll use to project the PowerPoint presentation.

Checking the Technology

Stories rely on a strong beginning to set the tone and direction of the rest of the narrative. Although you have a strong beginning built in to Act I of the story template, the presentation actually begins when the eyes of the audience turn to you and recognize you as the speaker. You're not off to a strong start if what they see is you connecting the projector cable to your computer, focusing the image on the screen, and searching for your PowerPoint file amid the clutter of your computer's desktop screen. Audiences are sometimes tolerant of these sorts of distractions, but you can't count on it. That's why you need to prepare for your technical needs in advance.

When you survey the room where you'll present, take the time to perform all of the steps it will take to set up the technology for the presentation. Plug the projector into the computer, power up the equipment, and open the PowerPoint file. Make any technical adjustments you need, and then resize the image to fit the screen and focus it. If you use a remote control device to advance the slides, try it out to make sure that it works properly. Test the Internet connection if you need one, and review any online materials you'll show on the projector during the presentation. If you plan to display Web pages, make a backup copy of them on your local computer in case you have problems with the Internet connection.

If you're not able to set up the equipment and rehearse in the room in advance of the presentation, at a minimum you should set up the equipment before the presentation with enough time available to resolve any technology issues that might arise. You might also want to rehearse in a similar room beforehand.

Planning for Problems

Even if something goes wrong, you can still produce a solid presentation experience. For example, if your speaking time is unexpectedly cut from 45 minutes to 15 or even 5 minutes, you can quickly scale the presentation to the reduced time by following the instructions in "Tip 2: Scale to Time," in Chapter 4. If your computer crashes and you have no way to recover it, you can still cover all of the presentation points by using a printout of the story template, storyboard, outline, notes pages, or slides. If the projector bulb burns out and you have no spare, your simple slides might be clear enough to be seen on the computer screen by a small audience at a table. Your thorough preparation will enable you to carry out the presentation with confidence, no matter what problems come your way.

Rehearsing Away Distractions

In the past, you might have waited until you had finished creating the slides before you rehearsed the presentation for the first time. But with the Beyond Bullet Points approach, you've already rehearsed at least five times. You get comfortable with your story when you read it aloud from the story template at three time lengths, as you did in Chapter 3. You become acquainted with the flow and sequence of the story when you rehearse from the storyboard headlines, as you did in Chapter 4. And you become familiar with seeing the visuals on screen when you rehearse using the completed slides, as you did in Chapter 6. Through each of these rehearsals, you address a number of possible distractions such as excess hand movement or over-reliance on notes or slides. Rehearsing helps you to remove distractions from the delivery of the presentation that come from being ill-prepared.

TIP   One effective technique to keep you focused during the rehearsal is to keep an image of the conclusion in mind. Review the Act III, Scene 3 slide, which is the slide you'll have on screen while you give the concluding remarks. Keep that image in your mind as you speak. Try beginning the rehearsal with the conclusion slide, and then proceed in sequence through the rest of the slides. Holding the image of the destination in mind can help you to stay focused on where you're going.

When you check the room and technology setup, stand in the physical location where you'll present and give a dress rehearsal of the presentation. Ask someone on your team to attend and give you honest feedback about the presentation, because you'll never improve unless someone suggests how you should. In the Contoso example, you would ask the Contoso CEO Chris Gray or other executives to sit in and offer you advice. Bring printouts of the notes pages for the attendees so that they can note suggested improvements on paper. You can incorporate their changes when you get back to the office.

TIP One of the best ways to become aware of your speaking mannerisms is to join a local speaking club such as Toastmasters International, described in "Tip 2: Toastmasters," later in this chapter. A good club offers you the opportunity to receive constructive feedback in a supportive environment—something most people don't get in the day-to-day context of their work.

People are inclined to mention only good things, so ask your evaluators not only to confirm what you do well, but also to suggest specific ways you can improve. It's a good idea to ask for a range of opinions because each viewer will give you advice from a different perspective. Take account of whatever feedback you get, and make adjustments as needed.

Using Notes

Although you should be intimately familiar with the presentation at this point, it's a good idea to keep a set of speaker notes on the podium in the form of a printed story template or storyboard outline. Don't use the complete notes pages as speaker notes—the written text in the notes area might tempt you to read from the page, and you'd need to physically flip from one page to the next, which would be distracting. Instead, when you print your key PowerPoint documents, consider using as speaker notes the story template, a text outline of the storyboard, or thumbnail images of the storyboard. To print these key documents, follow these steps.

TIP One of the most common verbal distractions is the use of filler words like *um, uh, I mean,* and *you know.* Most people aren't even aware that they use these words—even some of the most experienced speakers. To reduce distracting verbal fillers, record yourself when you speak so that you can listen to yourself and count the "ums." Or ask someone you know to count the number of filler word occurrences while you speak. The surest cure for this distracting habit is becoming aware that you do it in the first place.

To print your key PowerPoint documents

1 Open the Microsoft Word document that contains the story template. If you made any changes to the headlines in the storyboard, update the Word document to reflect those changes, and then print a copy.

2 To print a text outline of the storyboard, open the PowerPoint file, click **Print**, and in the **Print What** area of the **Print** dialog box, click **Outline**. Then click **OK**.

3 To print thumbnail images of the storyboard, click **Print**, and in the **Print What** area, click **Handouts** and click **6** or **9** in the drop-down list. Leave the **Print Hidden Slides** check box selected, and click **OK**.

4 To print handouts from notes pages, click **Print**, and in the **Print What** area, click **Notes Pages**. If you used hidden storyboard guides, clear the **Print Hidden Slides** check box, and then click **OK**. You can also print the individual slides one per page, but you should have enough material with just the thumbnail images of the storyboard and the notes page printouts.

5 While you're at it, print any additional handouts you'll reference during the presentation, such as Microsoft Visio diagrams or flow charts, Microsoft Excel spreadsheets, and detailed charts and graphs.

Once you've printed all of the documents, as shown in Figure 7-1, assemble and bind them in a folder so that you have them in a single place for reference.

TIP To customize handouts using thumbnail-size images of the storyboard, you can add a logo to the Handout Master by clicking **View, Master, Handout Master** and inserting the logo in the various handout configurations there. If you want more layout options than are available in the **Print Dialog** box, you can print your handouts in Microsoft Word instead. Click **File, Send To, Microsoft Office Word**, click one of the layout options in the **Send to Microsoft Office Word** dialog box, and then click **OK**.

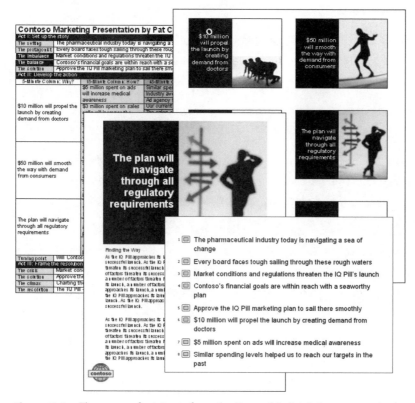

Figure 7-1 *The range of printouts from the Beyond Bullet Points approach.*

Developing a Dialog

When you made the audience the protagonist of your story in Act I of the story template, you made the story *all about them* instead of *all about you*. So rather than the presentation being a performance in which you're the star who entertains an adoring crowd, you're part of the supporting cast in the service of the audience. This is a shift from seeing the primary function of PowerPoint as *speaker support* to a new view in which PowerPoint serves as *audience support*.

A presentation isn't a one-way street; it takes the interaction of presenters and audiences to create a dialog. You just happen to be the first one to speak, and because you're the presenter, you're the one who is in charge of getting the interaction started.

Being Authentic

The dialog you create with the presentation begins with you—after all, the audience is granting you their time to listen to what you have to say. An audience will be more likely to give your presentation a fair hearing if they know that you're being authentic; you can convey this authenticity in a number of ways.

Adding your name to the byline of the story template when you begin writing the script establishes your personal responsibility for the presentation process from start to finish. The biggest benefit of being so closely involved is that the presentation eventually becomes an extension of who you are.

As you work on focusing the story in Act I and boiling down your ideas to three main points in Act II, you become increasingly confident with your message. Choosing a motif related to a personal interest helps you to express your personality and tap into your natural passion and excitement. And making creative choices for the design of the storyboard makes the PowerPoint presentation start to feel like an extension of your personality rather than a generic set of slides that everyone else uses.

One of the biggest obstacles you can impose on yourself when you speak in public is the idea that you need to be someone you're not. This problem becomes magnified if you're handed a generic corporate PowerPoint file with the same overstylized but boring look that everyone else uses. Although these presentations might look slick on the surface, they're often lacking the heart and soul that only the personality of a unique human being can bring.

You can break out of this trap using the new PowerPoint file you've created, which should reflect your character and personality in the choices you make for the story and visuals. Now you can expand on that personal beginning by delivering a presentation that expresses your original voice. Audiences will always prefer a presentation that's imperfect and a little rough around the edges—but still authentic—over a perfect and flawless presentation that has no soul.

When you present, never be afraid to be yourself, because that's what people really want you to be.

Working Confidently with Your Slides

For many people, the thought of public speaking inspires fear, not confidence. The fear often comes from speakers not being comfortable with their story, with themselves, or with their level of preparedness. You remove the elements that create fear by securing a strong story, extending your personality through the story, and rehearsing thoroughly along the way. Your confidence comes shining through most clearly in the way you use the projected slides you designed in Chapters 5 and 6.

After working with the PowerPoint file in Notes Page, Normal, and Slide Sorter views, you should be very comfortable with the material. When you advance to a new slide in the presentation, that slide's headline will prompt you about what to say next. The headline also addresses the audience in a conversational tone, making them feel relaxed and helping them to easily understand what you want to convey at that point.

Next on the slide is the graphical element. One of the benefits of the simplified design approach described in Chapters 5 and 6 is that the slides are free of bullet points and excess clutter; instead, you show a meaningful headline illustrated by a simple graphic. The goal of simple slides like these is to inspire interdependence between you and the audience. By showing less on screen, you pique the audience's curiosity.

Next you answer the audience's question about the slide with your spoken words, which you developed fully in the written explanation of each slide in the notes area. You explain the meaning of the headline and graphic to the audience in your own natural voice.

These three basic elements—headline, graphic, and your voice—work together to create an implicit dialog that engages the audience. When you finish the thought at hand, you advance to the next slide and repeat the process in a steady flow that naturally continues the dialog.

With the new PowerPoint presentation, you'll gain the focused attention of the audience through your relaxed approach, interesting story, and engaging visuals. Scan the room as you speak, making direct eye contact with audience members in every part of the room. Watch their faces to see how they're responding to the presentation. If people are fidgeting or restless, you might need to turn up your enthusiasm and speaking level.

Enlivening the Dialog

A presentation is a living experience, and you can amplify the life in the room by using a range of old and new techniques to help the audience feel even more involved in the dialog. One of the oldest and simplest techniques is to ask a question. This is especially useful in the first scenes of Act I, when you make an initial connection with the audience.

For example, in the Contoso presentation, the first headline is *The pharmaceutical industry today is navigating a sea of change*. When you show this slide, you could ask the question "How many of you agree that the industry is changing?" While asking a question that requires a poll of the audience, hold up your hand up to signal the audience to raise their hands. Then quickly count the number of hands and tell the audience the results of the poll as you move on to the next point, "It looks like about two-thirds of you agree. Well today we're going to talk about..." Taking a quick poll like this makes the audience feel like they're part of the conversation and also gives you a gauge of where the audience stands in relation to the topic.

You can vary this technique by using an interactive polling device, which some companies build specifically for PowerPoint. You could also experiment by hiding the headlines, as described in the section "Hiding the Headlines," in Chapter 5, and asking the question with only a graphic displayed. Asking a question with only a graphic on screen often works well because people bring their own meaning to the image. Again, this gives the audience a chance to participate in the conversation and allows them to be creative in their responses.

Handling Q & A

If you've done your work well in the story template, you anticipate questions by tailoring the presentation to the audience and addressing the questions they're wondering as you complete each of the acts and scenes. After you conclude your prepared remarks and invite audience comments, you'll have the opportunity to clear up any issues you might have missed. Opening the floor to Q & A is important—even if you've covered everything, people who are making decisions will still want to ask questions so that they feel like they've participated in the experience. In some instances, you may even want to purposely leave a few questions unanswered so the audience will be sure to ask them and engage you in the Q & A.

When you arrive at the resolution of the presentation in Act III, Scene 4 of the storyboard, leave this slide on the screen while you open the floor to questions. If you're speaking to a large audience and take a question, restate the question before you answer it to make sure that everyone in the room hears it.

If someone wants to ask a question about a particular slide, you can refer to the printed storyboard for the corresponding slide number to the left of the headline and then type the number of the slide and press **Enter** to go directly to that slide. If you want to show a slide that relates to a general question from one of the Act II scenes, type the number of whichever Act II slide corresponds with the question and press **Enter**. If you have extra material that didn't fit into the Act II slides but you think you might still be asked about it, add the extra slides to the end of the presentation and refer to them if some questions relate to them.

TIP   As an advanced technique, you can try using the PowerPoint storyboard on screen as a navigational aid. Before you start your presentation, go to Slide Sorter view and display the storyboard at a size that lets you see all of the slides at once—say, 33 percent. Leave the presentation in this view, and when you're ready to present, click **View**, **Slide Show** or press **F5** to begin. At the end of the presentation, press **Esc** to return to Slide Sorter view. This creates an interesting visual, and because you know the storyboard so well, when someone asks a question about a slide, you can click the slide to go directly to it.

Improvising Within Constraints

Because your new PowerPoint file is such a versatile platform, you can try endless improvisation with it as long as you follow the basic Beyond Bullet Points approach and stick to the ground rules. Following these rules keeps the presentation firmly rooted while leaving your creative options open to try new things.

Keeping Control of Your Story

Because of your relaxed approach, you might find that people ask you questions during the presentation or offer stories of their own experiences. This is a good sign that the audience is feeling comfortable with your speaking style. Unfortunately, these queries can also cause you to head off on a tangent that throws off your timing and story structure. Handle questions graciously by quickly answering them if you can, or by acknowledging them and deferring them to the Q & A session at the end of the presentation. If you don't know the answer to a question, admit that you don't know, and offer to follow up on the matter later.

It's essential to stay on course with your story; if you don't, you can easily lose control of the situation. The goal of the Beyond Bullet Points approach is to create a compelling story that's tailored to the audience and anticipates their questions so that they're completely absorbed to the very end. If you missed the mark and your story wasn't a good fit for the audience, spend time after the presentation reviewing the story template so that you can improve the next story you write. Pay particular attention to the Act I scenes to ensure that the story engages the audience fully.

If you need flexibility, you can always jump ahead to any point in a presentation by typing the number of a slide and pressing **Enter**. At a minimum, you should cover all of Act I, the first slide in each scene in Act II, and all of Act III, because they form the essential structure of your story.

Preparing for Different Contexts

The Beyond Bullet Points approach is based on a time-tested classical story structure that should appeal to anyone, so you should be able to use the same approach for audiences of different sizes.

For most audiences, a large screen is ample for projecting a presentation; for large audiences, the screen needs to be large enough for the people in the back row to see the slides clearly. A large audience size usually prevents you from getting feedback while you're presenting, but that doesn't prevent the experience from being an implicit dialog, as described earlier in this chapter.

For an audience of one or two people, you can give the presentation using a laptop with a large screen, printouts of the slides, or even a handheld computer. In each of these cases, you lose the power of a large projected image, but you gain in terms of a more casual and conversational approach and the immediacy of starting right away with little or no need to deal with technology setup.

Turning Off Your Slides

One of the most powerful and effective improvisation techniques is to simply black out the screen during the presentation. Visuals projected on a screen can be spellbinding, but when you break that spell by blacking out the screen, you focus the audience's attention completely on you and your ideas at a specific moment. This creates an abrupt shift in the presentation that you can use to dramatic effect to emphasize an important point.

To apply this technique to emphasize the point of a key slide in the presentation, locate the slide in Slide Sorter view. Right-click the slide, and on the shortcut menu, click **Background**. In the **Background** dialog box, click the **Background Color** drop-down arrow and click black. Click the title area, and on the **Formatting** toolbar, click the **Font Color** drop-down arrow and click black, if it is not already selected. Remove any other elements on the slide. (If you apply this technique during the design phase of the presentation, you won't need to find a graphical element for the slide.)

When you return to Slide Sorter view, you can see the position of the black slide between the two slides on either side of it, so you can plan what you will say across the sequence of slides. During the presentation, advance your slides as usual, but when the black slide appears, pause for effect and make your point while the audience focuses on you. Then advance to the next slide to resume the sequence of visible slides.

Alternatively, if you want to black out any slide during a presentation, press **B** to turn the screen black (or **W** to turn it white). When you press the same key again, you'll return to the same visible slide. The tradeoffs with this technique are that you won't be able to see the blacked out slide in Slide Sorter view to plan for it in the storyboard, and when you press the **B** or **W** key again, you return to the same slide rather than the next one in the presentation.

Handing Out Handouts

Many presenters find it best to provide handouts after the presentation to prevent distractions. On the other hand, many audiences ask for handouts because they like to make notes on paper during a presentation. Try both approaches to see what works best for you and your audiences. One compromise is to print and hand out in advance a one-page version of the story template so that the audience has a basic road map of where you're going. You can mention at the beginning of the presentation that you'll provide comprehensive handouts at the end, and at that point provide sets of handouts in the form of printed notes pages.

Presenting Without Being Present

If you can't present in person, you obviously miss out on the kind of communication that happens only in a live environment. But that doesn't have to stop you from presenting when you're not physically present—you just need to configure the PowerPoint presentation differently.

Sending Your Notes Pages (Not Your Slides)

When you added graphics to the presentation in Chapters 5 and 6, you learned that the slides prepared using the Beyond Bullet Points approach don't make much sense unless you look at them in Notes Page view. The same holds true if you want to send the PowerPoint presentation to someone who couldn't attend the presentation in person, so never send just the slides—always send the notes pages.

Handouts in the form of notes pages offer quick reading as a printed document. Readers can quickly understand the main idea of the document by skimming headlines and visuals from page to page, and they can also spend more time reading narrative detail in the notes area if they want.

REMEMBER If you want to send a PowerPoint file to someone who wasn't at the presentation, don't send the slides, send the notes pages instead.

An effective way to send notes pages is in Adobe Acrobat PDF file format. When you e-mail the notes pages in this format, the audience has access to all of the information you want to present, but not access to the original PowerPoint file where you keep the graphical materials and editable text you might not want to make available.

Producing an Online Presentation

When you can't be there in person, you can instead display the presentation on a Web browser. The PowerPoint presentation message will work well in the Web browser context, because the same engaging story structure is there. The same simple visuals that support interdependence with your spoken words are there too, as well as the same evenly sized chunks of information, the same even pacing, and the same even flow.

The simplest way to put a presentation online is to post an Adobe PDF file of the notes pages on a Web site. Or you can convert the presentation to an online format using a conversion tool that allows you to record your narration as you display the slides. Many technologies are available, such as Microsoft Producer and Microsoft Office Live Meeting, that can easily and quickly transform the presentation into an online format. With most of these tools, the slides are displayed in a browser, and you use a microphone to record what you've written in the notes area. When the audience views the slides, they hear your spoken narration through their computers. Some online technology solutions also make the notes area viewable, in case people prefer to quickly scan what you're saying and skip ahead.

And Now Presenting...

You should now be ready to present to the Contoso board of directors—or to any audience, for that matter. With the thorough presentation you've prepared using the Beyond Bullet Points approach, you're sure to persuade the audience with your focused, clear, and engaging story.

As you apply this system to other presentations, keep this book handy, and visit the Beyond Bullets blog, described in "Tip 10: Stay in Touch Using the Beyond Bullets Blog," later in this chapter, to get a steady supply of ideas.

Before you give the presentation, review the following 10 tips to find ideas to spark your imagination or inspire you to try something new.

10 Tips for Enhancing Your Production

You now have a flexible and robust system for bringing your ideas to life using PowerPoint. You can keep building on this foundation by using these 10 tips to bring your ideas to life.

Tip 1: The Living Brand

In the conventional bullet points approach, it's common for presenters to place a logo on the Slide Master in an effort to ensure that the visual stamp of an organization is on every slide. But the Beyond Bullet Points approach uses a different set of techniques to ensure that an organization's identity is carried through presentations.

Instead of placing a logo on the Slide Master, you place the logo on the Notes Master, for a number of reasons. Removing the logo from the screen aligns with the *coherence principle*, described in Appendix A, which is based on research that indicates that putting extraneous information on a screen can distract from the audience's ability to understand the point at hand. Eliminating the logo from the Slide Master increases the amount of screen real estate available for presenting information and opens up the many creative options that an empty screen allows. And keeping the screen clear of a logo removes an obstacle that would stand in the way of the audience becoming completely absorbed in a story; it would be distracting if you went to see a film and an entertainment company's logo was prominently displayed in the corner of the screen.

But beyond those reasons, in a live presentation context, the concept of a visual stamp on a slide diminishes in importance because all eyes are on you, and you are actually *living the brand*. The high quality of your ideas, the compelling story, the interesting visuals, and the high level of engagement all contribute to an experience that the audience will not soon forget. And just in case they do, they'll always have the handout, which includes your logo on the notes pages.

Tip 2: Toastmasters

If you're not a member of a speaking club, you should be. Any speaker can benefit from attending a regular meeting with the sole purpose of improving a full range of speaking skills. Toastmasters International, at *www.toastmasters.org*, is a good choice because it's inexpensive and all clubs are run by the volunteer efforts of their members. When you join, you'll participate in speaking exercises during meetings and give a series of prepared talks according to a sequence in a training manual.

The biggest benefits will likely come from simply attending regularly. As you're exposed to more speaking opportunities in a supportive environment, you'll develop skills to manage your nervousness, and your confidence will increase not just in public speaking but in all aspects of communications.

Many clubs haven't yet embraced the use of presentation technologies. If your local club doesn't yet use PowerPoint, bring a data projector and introduce some of the ideas you've picked up in this book to blend projected media and solid speaking skills.

Tip 3: Stretch Yourself

A live presentation draws on the full spectrum of communication skills, but almost no one is good at everything. You're probably better at one part of the presentation process—for example, writing your story, editing your headlines, boiling down your ideas, checking your reasoning, creating visuals, or actually speaking and presenting. When you know your strength, pick a different area to work on improving. For example, if you're good at writing, learn graphics, or if you're good at graphics, work on your public speaking. Only by stretching can you keep on growing.

Tip 4: Preparing Your Introduction

One of the most overlooked parts of the presentation experience is the set of words that introduces you before you stand up to speak. A good introduction raises an audience's interest in the presentation and establishes your authority to give the talk in the first place. To make sure that your story gets off to a solid start, plan the way you'll be introduced. Write a brief description of you and your talk that the introducer can use as an outline.

As you write this description, keep the Act I scenes in mind, and think of a brief way to set up this story that you're about to tell. Also be sure to describe your credentials as they relate to the topic of the presentation. This isn't just tooting your own horn—to be in the right frame of mind to listen to the presentation, the audience needs to know that you're the right person to be giving this talk.

Tip 5: Got Gobo?

Many standard meeting rooms feature fluorescent lights and ordinary tables, but with inexpensive lighting tools, you can change the atmosphere of the room to remove the distractions of a shabby presentation environment. For example, a simple way to light up the presentation environment is with a *gobo*, which is a partial screen with the cutout of a pattern that's placed over a light. When you turn on the light, it projects the image of the pattern onto a surface. You could use a gobo to project a subtle pattern to cover up an uneven wall or to add a soft color to make glaring lights less obvious. As with all of the visuals you've prepared for the presentation, any visual effects should be transparent and never distract from the message. If you've "got gobo," or any other special lighting, keep in mind that people should remember the message and not the lighting.

Tip 6: Visual Mnemonics

Having problems trying to remember what you want to say? Try using the slides to trigger your memory about key points. For example, if you display the visual prop of a ship's wheel, shown in Figure 7-2, and you plan to make six key points in the presentation, you can associate each point with one of the handles of the wheel, speaking about each one as you follow the handles around.

Figure 7-2   *Using a simple photograph as a visual mnemonic.*

When you use an image on a slide as a visual mnemonic, you can make your ideas, as well as the presentation, memorable.

Tip 7: Make the Conversation High Voltage

In *Moving Mountains* (Crowell-Collier Press, 1989), Henry M. Boettinger wrote, "Presentation of ideas is conversation carried on at high voltage—at once more dangerous and more powerful." This is one of the best definitions of presentations because it packs so much meaning into a brief sentence, which becomes even more meaningful when it's broken up into pieces:

- You're presenting *ideas*. Not your ego.

- A presentation is a *conversation*. There are at least two people involved.

- A presentation is *high voltage*. It's not boring.

- A presentation is *dangerous*. It's risky.

- A presentation is *powerful*. It has strength.

The next time you speak, keep Boettinger's wise definition in mind to stay focused on the meaning you pack into your presentations.

Tip 8: Magnify Intimacy

One of the most powerful techniques in film is magnifying the face of an actor to give the audience a feeling of intimacy with that person. Although you won't see that technique in most presentations, new technologies continue to transform the presentation landscape.

For example, in some presentations, an IMAG image magnification camera will zoom in on a presenter's face while he or she is speaking at a live event. The image is often featured in a split screen format next to the speaker's PowerPoint slides on a wide screen. If you have the chance to have your face magnified on a screen, embrace the opportunity—you're giving the audience a chance to see you up close. But before you do, you should sign up for media training using a live camera similar to the one in the presentation so that you can see how you look on the big screen.

Tip 9: Script Multiple Speakers

When you have multiple people speaking about one story, use the story template to plan what each speaker will say.

To do this, write the complete and single story as you did in Chapters 2 and 3. When it's time to deliver the presentations, Speaker 1 presents the Act I scenes to introduce the story. Speaker 2 presents the series of slides in Act II, Scene 1; Speaker 3 presents the series of slides in Act II, Scene 2; and Speaker 4 presents the series of slides in Act II, Scenes 3 and 4. Then Speaker 1 returns to tie everything together in the Act III scenes.

Whether you use this technique for a small meeting or for a large conference, it ensures that the audience experiences a single story that makes sense to them. You should also send the storyboards for each section to the speakers to design in advance; this ensures that all of the speakers stay on message and also project their own unique styles and personalities.

Tip 10: Stay in Touch Using the Beyond Bullets Blog

Many of the ideas in this book were inspired by the Beyond Bullets blog, at *www.beyondbullets.com*. This blog features a steady supply of tips, techniques, and creative ideas for presentations. Like the "10 Tips" sections at the end of each chapter in this book, each blog entry features an advanced idea you can apply to your PowerPoint presentations using the Beyond Bullet Points approach. If you'd like to stay connected, subscribe to this free service to keep the fresh ideas coming, and be sure to send your own ideas and innovations to share with other readers and presenters.

Conclusion

To answer the question first posed in the introduction to this book: *Of course* a Microsoft Office PowerPoint presentation without bullet points is still a PowerPoint presentation. In fact, it might be even more than you imagined a presentation could be.

In less than 20 years, PowerPoint has changed how we communicate in ways that have gone largely unrecognized and unheralded. Just as the arrival of television changed the configuration of our living rooms, the arrival of PowerPoint and data projectors has changed the configuration of our meeting rooms. In both situations, the screen is the center of attention. But where television is still essentially a one-way medium, PowerPoint puts in your hand a tool that you can choose to turn on, pause, interact with, or turn off to create a dialog with an audience.

To some extent, the popularity of PowerPoint software is tied to deeper changes at work in our global culture, including a rapid shift from using text as the primary mode of communication to using multimedia as the preferred mode. This can be seen in many organizations in which PowerPoint has eclipsed the written word as the primary means by which people communicate with one another. Significantly, all of this has been accomplished *in spite of* the conventional bullet points approach that many people say creates a wall between presenters and audiences. In this light, we can look forward to seeing what happens to the PowerPoint landscape when the wall falls down and people start moving beyond bullet points.

When you apply the power of a persuasive story structure to your entire presentation-making process, as described in this book, you do much more than create a presentation. You actually break the mold of traditional interpersonal communications by blending your message with digital media in a live conversation with an audience. It's not just about what you say or how you say it anymore—it's about *combining* the what and how in a way that sparks a dialog with other people over your ideas. This is an exciting development in the history of communication, and it makes you a pioneer forging past the old models of mass media into a new world of much more sociable media.

There's always cultural resistance to new ideas, just as there will be to the idea of moving beyond bullet points. This is especially the case when you're engaging with PowerPoint-related issues at the organizational level. When you see PowerPoint presentations, you see a reflection of an organization's culture, and some cultures are resistant to change. If you run into resistance, don't be discouraged. The power of media has been put in the hands of the people by the widespread availability of PowerPoint, and it's not going back. As presenters use this tool to express themselves and engage other people, there's no stopping the positive changes that are bound to occur.

The end of this book is really just the beginning. As the word *beyond* in the title implies, this book's intent is to move in a new direction, outside the constraints of bullet points and into a new world of focus, clarity, and engagement. When the bullet points begin to fall from our PowerPoint slides, we'll find that we can once again see one another and begin a conversation. And as we blend our good ideas with the powerful media technologies available today, the state of interpersonal communications will evolve to a much more engaging and human level.

In a Beyond Bullet Points world, there's no stopping the power of the human story.

Appendix A: **Aligning with the Research**

Although the conventional bullet points approach has become the norm for communicating in presentations, you might be surprised to learn that little research has been conducted on its effectiveness. Anecdotes abound in the popular press and in practitioner journals about the shortcomings of bullet points on presentation screens, suggesting a need for further research by organizations and educators who use this approach.

One reason for the lack of research on the bullet points approach might be the speed at which this approach has been adopted and propagated through organizations and classrooms, leaving little time for reflection and analysis. Another reason might be that studying a live presentation environment is difficult because it involves many variables, including the quality of the presentation media, the communication skills of the presenter, and the comprehension level of the audience.

Although little research focuses specifically on the effectiveness of the conventional bullet points approach, one promising area of research relates to other approaches that use multimedia to support learning. This research relates to the *cognitive theory of multimedia learning* proposed by educational psychologist Richard E. Mayer, Ph.D., a professor of psychology at the University of California, Santa Barbara. Ranked by a national study as the most prolific researcher in the field of educational psychology, Mayer is the author of 18 books and more than 250 articles and chapters, and has been researching multimedia learning and problem solving for 12 years.

Mayer's approach doesn't begin by asking how any specific software tool can best be used for any purpose; instead, it begins by asking how the human mind works. With that understanding of the human mind established, the research examines principles that can guide any approach that uses multimedia to enhance effective learning.

One of the most important assumptions of research in this area is the idea that the human mind is an active participant in the process of learning. This is a big shift from the assumption that the minds of audiences are passive vessels waiting to be filled by a presenter's knowledge. If we think that people will "get" what we want to communicate just because we show them slides filled with bullet points, we're making an assumption that doesn't line up with the most current thinking in cognitive theory.

Reviewing Mayer's Research-Based Principles

In his important book *Multimedia Learning* (Cambridge University Press, 2001), and in related articles and papers, Mayer proposes a way to understand the use of multimedia that promotes meaningful learning and lays out a set of principles for designing any multimedia experience based on his own research and that of others.

Mayer's principles offer a way to align your approach to Microsoft Office PowerPoint presentations with the way the human mind works. The principles also provide important criteria to help you to choose which graphical techniques to use and which to discard.

When you use the approach described in this book, you've already gone a long way toward aligning with many of these design principles described in Mayer's work, as described in the following sections.

Communicating with Words and Pictures

As you saw in the section "Rule 1: Design the Complete Experience Around the Headline," in Chapter 5, you begin the process of designing your presentation in Notes Page view. Your design task is to place a graphic in the slide area to fill the blank space between the headline that appears on screen and the notes area that contains the narration you read aloud, as shown in Figure A-1. You add the graphic to the slide in Normal view, and you apply this technique to every slide in the presentation. This ensures that every graphic is directly relevant to the idea explained by the headline and the notes area—not added just for decoration.

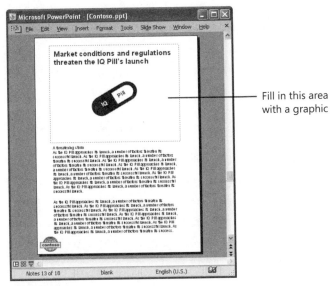

Figure A-1 *Notes Page view ensuring that you communicate with both words and pictures, and that most words are narrated rather than placed on screen.*

Ensuring that every slide in the presentation contains a visual that is directly related to the idea at hand aligns your approach with Mayer's *multimedia principle,* which states that people learn better from words and pictures than from words alone.

Avoiding the Redundancy of Narration and On-Screen Text

Beginning in Notes Page view ensures that you design each notes page as an integrated media document, as shown in Figure A-1. Because every slide in the presentation contains a visual, you always have a graphic in the slide area. This integrated approach eliminates the need to place any information that you'll provide in your spoken narration in the slide area.

Keeping text mostly in the notes area and the slide area free of bullet points aligns your approach with Mayer's *redundancy principle,* which states that people understand a multimedia explanation better when the words are presented as verbal narration alone, instead of both verbally and as on-screen text.

In some cases, verbal redundancy might be acceptable—for example, when the pace of the presentation is especially slow, when you're introducing technical terms that are new to the audience, or when audience members might have difficulty understanding the presentation because they're not native speakers or they have hearing problems.

Keeping Information in Bite-Sized Segments

When you complete the story template, as you did in Chapters 2 and 3, you break up the information in your story into chunks in the form of individual statements. These chunks of information fit into the clear structure and sequence of the story template that form the foundation of the presentation. You then transfer the story template to PowerPoint, where each statement is placed in the title area of its own slide, as shown in Slide Sorter view in Figure A-2.

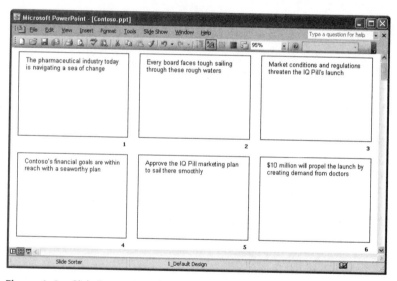

Figure A-2   *Slide Sorter view showing information that has been broken into one chunk per slide.*

Breaking information into chunks in the story template and then placing one chunk per slide aligns your approach with Mayer's *segmentation principle*, which states that people learn better when information is presented in bite-size segments.

Clearly Signaling Information

When you send the statements from the story template to a PowerPoint file, as you did in the section "Transferring Your Script to PowerPoint," in Chapter 4, each statement is placed in the title area of each slide, and you can read across the headlines in Slide Sorter view, as shown in Figure A-3.

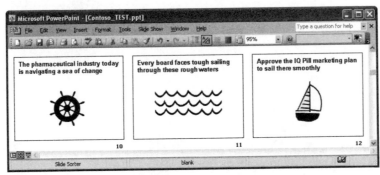

Figure A-3   *Slide Master indicating a layout with a headline that clearly explains the idea at hand.*

Placing a clear headline on each slide aligns your approach with Mayer's *signaling principle*, which states that people learn better when information is presented using clear outlines and headings.

If you send a headline to the back of a photograph, as described in the section "Hiding the Headlines," in Chapter 5, the headline no longer signals the meaning of your slide. You might be able to compensate for the loss of signaling by emphasizing your point through your motif, the visual, and your spoken words.

Using a Conversational Style

When you write the statements of the story template by following the guideline in the section "Rule 2: Use a Conversational Tone That Is Simple, Clear, and Direct," in Chapter 2, you ensure that the headlines of the slides are complete sentences that convey a conversational tone, as shown in Figure A-4.

Using a conversational style for the headlines aligns your approach with Mayer's *personalization principle*, which states that people learn better when information is presented in a conversational style rather than a formal one.

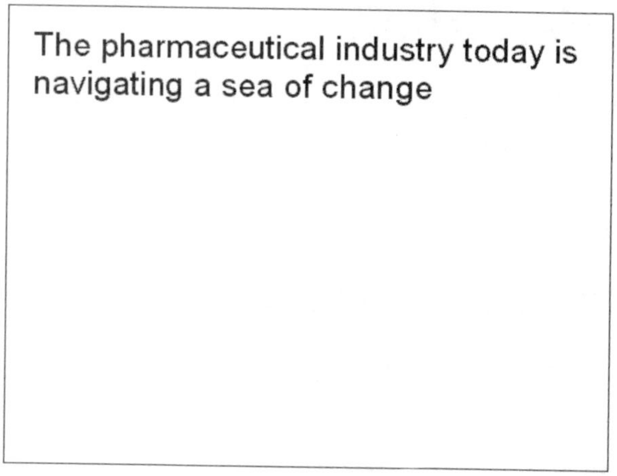

The pharmaceutical industry today is navigating a sea of change

Figure A-4 *A headline with a conversational tone, supporting the personalization principle.*

Placing Headlines Near Graphics

By reformatting all of the slides with a Title and Content layout, as you did in the section "Changing the Slide Layout," in Chapter 4, you create a default layout that places a meaningful headline at the top of the slide and a visual element in the area below, as shown in Figure A-5.

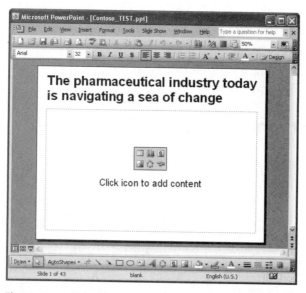

Figure A-5 *Title and Content layout ensuring that the headline and graphics are placed close to one another.*

Using the Title and Content layout aligns your approach with Mayer's *spatial contiguity principle*, which states that people learn better when words are presented near the corresponding pictures rather than far from them on a screen or page. Labels and pointers can be added to the graphical elements if needed to further clarify them, as shown in Chapter 6 in Figure 6-1.

Keeping the Screen Clear of Distractions

In the section "Setting Up the Slide Master," in Chapter 4, you deleted the Date, Footer, and Number areas, left the slide background blank, and didn't add a logo or any other design elements, as shown in Figure A-6. This technique creates a clear and simple master from which you can begin working with your slides.

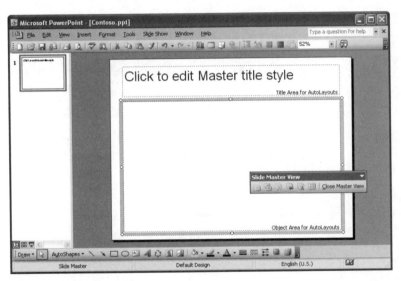

Figure A-6 *A blank background removes distracting graphical elements from the screen.*

Beginning the design process with a blank slide that is clear of graphical elements aligns your approach with Mayer's *coherence principle*, which states that people learn better when extraneous information is removed from a multimedia presentation.

This important principle is based on research that shows that learning can be hindered when you add interesting but irrelevant words, pictures, sounds, and music to a presentation. You reinforce this principle when you strictly limit what's placed in the slide area to only graphics that directly relate to the headline and the notes area, as mentioned earlier in the *multimedia principle*. You also adhere to this principle by keeping the slide layout basic, the style of graphical elements simple, and the design of diagrams and charts free of unnecessary ornamentation.

Narrating Animated Elements

By designing a sequence of related statements in the story template, as described in the section "Explaining an Idea Using a Diagram" in Chapter 5, you build an animation over a sequence of slides similar to the frames in a film, as shown in Figure A-7. Because the narration is captured in the notes area below each slide, there's no need to clutter the slide area with additional text that explains each visual element.

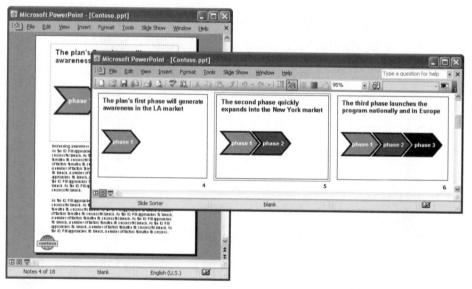

Figure A-7   *Diagram animation sequence that ensures narration for each animated element.*

Addressing your narrated words in the notes area and keeping them off screen aligns your approach with Mayer's *modality principle*, which states that people learn better from animation and narration than from animation with explanatory on-screen text. This principle is especially important in fast-paced presentations. In some instances, the addition of labels can help to clarify technical terms.

Synchronizing Animation and Narration

By creating an animation sequence from a series of slides that is also linked to the narration in the notes area, as described in the section "Explaining an Idea Across Slides Using a Chart," in Chapter 5, you ensure that you narrate each step in sequence, as shown in Figure A-8.

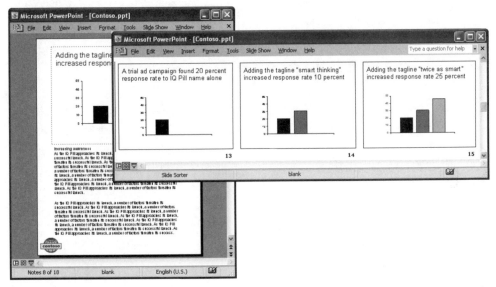

Figure A-8 *Chart animation sequence ensuring that animation and narration are synchronized.*

Synchronizing narration in the notes area with each frame of animation in the slide area aligns with Mayer's *temporal contiguity principle*, which states that people learn better when animation and narration are presented simultaneously rather than successively.

Applying Advanced Principles

These principles cover the basics for general audiences whose background details you don't know in advance. Once you master this approach and if know the background of your audience more thoroughly, you can tailor the words and images to meet the individual needs of specific audiences by applying advanced principles.

For example, a category of learning differences among people relates to prior knowledge, visual literacy, and spatial aptitude. Mayer's *individual differences principle* states that the design of multimedia presentations can have different effects based on each of these factors. For example, you could use a complex diagram to illustrate a single slide if everyone in the audience has prior knowledge of it; you'd explain the same diagram over a sequence of slides if the audience is new to the information. For more information on these advanced principles, refer to the additional resources below.

Learning More About the Research

If you're interested in learning more about the research work of Mayer and others and how to apply it to your presentations, refer to the following list of resources. As you begin to apply the approach described in this book, keep in mind that you're helping to develop an innovative new approach to multimedia presentations that's still in a relatively early stage of evolution. You can use the Beyond Bullet Points approach to build your presentations on a strong foundation that aligns with many of the research-based principles described here, and as a solid starting point for further experimentation and research.

Additional Resources

- *Multimedia Learning*, by Richard E. Mayer (Cambridge University Press, 2001)

- *Nine Ways to Reduce Cognitive Load in Multimedia Learning*, by Richard E. Mayer and Roxana Moreno (*Educational Psychologist*, 38, no. 1 [2003])

- *The Cognitive Load of PowerPoint: Q&A with Richard E. Mayer*, by Cliff Atkinson, March 2004, *www.sociablemedia.com/articles_mayer.htm*

- *Five Ways to Reduce PowerPoint Overload*, by Richard E. Mayer and Cliff Atkinson, *www.sociablemedia.com*

- *Graphics for Learning: Proven Guidelines for Planning, Designing, and Evaluating Visuals in Training Materials*, by Ruth Colvin Clark and Chopeta Lyons (Pfeiffer, 2004)

Appendix B: **Using the Storyboard Formatter**

The Beyond Bullet Points Storyboard Formatter is a Microsoft PowerPoint file that you can use to save time reformatting the Slide Master and Notes Master, as described "Setting Up the Slide Master" and "Setting Up the Notes Master," in Chapter 4. It also includes a set of predesigned Beyond Bullet Points Storyboard Guides for your use, as described in "Creating Storyboard Guides," in Chapter 4.

You can download the Storyboard Formatter from the Beyond Bullet Points book resource section at *www.sociablemedia.com*, and save it to your local computer.

To use the Beyond Bullet Points Storyboard Formatter

1   Follow the steps in the section "Sending the Story Template from Word to PowerPoint," in Chapter 4 to create a new PowerPoint file that you save on your local computer.

2   In Slide Sorter view, click **Edit**, **Select All**, and on the **Standard** toolbar, click the **Copy** button.

3   Locate the Beyond Bullet Points Storyboard Formatter on your local computer, and double-click it. Because the file format is a PowerPoint Design Template, indicated by a .pot file extension, double-clicking the file will open a new presentation based on the template's formatting. Name and save the new PowerPoint file on your local computer.

4   Position the cursor to the left of the first slide, and on the **Standard** toolbar, click the **Paste** button, and then save the file. All of the slides from the PowerPoint file you created in step 1 will now be formatted properly according to the procedures described in the sections "Setting Up the Slide Master" and "Setting Up the Notes Master," in Chapter 4.

5 Click **Edit**, **Select All**, click **Format**, **Slide Layout**, and click the **Title and Content** layout to apply it to all of the selected slides. (If you prefer a simpler layout, click the **Title Only** layout instead.)

6 To arrange the hidden storyboard guides included in the Storyboard Formatter, follow the steps in the section "To Reposition the Storyboard Guides," in Chapter 4. If you use the optional 45 Minutes and 15 Minutes storyboard guides, duplicate and position them according to the instructions in "Tip 2: Scale to Time," in Chapter 4.

Installing the Storyboard Formatter as the Default for New Presentations

If you want to make the Beyond Bullet Points Storyboard Formatter the default that opens every time you create a new PowerPoint file, you can save it to your local computer as the default template. Doing this saves time because every new presentation you generate is preformatted. Before you follow these steps, confirm that you want to overwrite the existing default PowerPoint template, which you can preview by clicking the **New** button on the **Standard** toolbar.

To install the Beyond Bullet Points Storyboard Formatter

1 Double-click the Beyond Bullet Points Storyboard Formatter to open it. Click **File**, **Save As**, and in the **Save As** dialog box, click the **Save As Type** drop-down arrow, and choose **Design Template (*.pot)**. PowerPoint automatically selects the location on your local computer where the default PowerPoint template is stored.

2 In the list of filenames that appears, double-click **default.pot** or, if it's missing, double-click **blank.pot**. A warning appears to ask whether you want to replace the existing file; click **Yes**. This overwrites the existing default template on your computer.

3 To create a new presentation, on the **Standard** toolbar, click the **New** button, which will open a new PowerPoint file that has been preformatted using the Storyboard Formatter. Then follow the steps in "To Use the Beyond Bullet Points Storyboard Formatter," earlier in this appendix, except skip step 3 because you already have a preformatted presentation open.

If you want to modify the Storyboard Formatter, refer to "Tip 7: Customize the Beyond Bullet Points Storyboard Formatter," in Chapter 4.

Index

What do you think of this book? We want to hear from you!

Do you have a few minutes to participate in a brief online survey? Microsoft is interested in hearing your feedback about this publication so that we can continually improve our books and learning resources for you.

To participate in our survey, please visit:

www.microsoft.com/learning/booksurvey

And enter this book's ISBN, 0-7356-2052-0. As a thank-you to survey participants in the United States and Canada, each month we'll randomly select five respondents to win one of five $100 gift certificates from a leading online merchant.* At the conclusion of the survey, you can enter the drawing by providing your e-mail address, which will be used for prize notification *only*.

Thanks in advance for your input. Your opinion counts!

Sincerely,

Microsoft Learning

Learn More. Go Further.

To see special offers on Microsoft Learning products for developers, IT professionals, and home and office users, visit: *www.microsoft.com/learning/booksurvey*

* No purchase necessary. Void where prohibited. Open only to residents of the 50 United States (includes District of Columbia) and Canada (void in Quebec). Sweepstakes ends 6/30/2005. For official rules, see: *www.microsoft.com/learning/booksurvey*